need to know?

Jazz

Bob Blumenthal

First published in 2007 by Collins
an imprint of
HarperCollins Publishers
77–85 Fulham Palace Road
London W6 8JB

www.collins.co.uk

Collins is a registered trademark of HarperCollins Publis

A catalogue record for this book is available from the British
Library

ISBN-13: 978-0-00-724390-7

Captions for pictures opening each chapter
p.12. Composer and pianist Jelly Roll Morton in a contemplative
moment.
p.30. Thanks to the microphone, jazz became widely
disseminated via both the phonograph recording and the radio
broadcast.
p.72. Bebop in its heyday on Manhattan's 52nd Street in the
late 1940s. Among those pictured are trumpeter Fats Navarro,
pianist Tadd Dameron and drummer Kenny Clarke.
p.126. Trombonist Grachan Moncur III and tenor saxophonist
Archie Shepp were among those representing the freedom
wing of jazz in the 1960s.
p.160. Pianist Brad Mehldau is one of the young musicians in
the lead as jazz enters a new century.

Back cover photos
© Orlando Barria/epa/Corbis – image of Trombone player and
the sunset – middle.
© Bettmann/CORBIS – image of Bing Crosby – right.
© Christopher Felver/Corbis – Branford Marsalis – left.

Smithsonian consultant: John Edward Hasse, Smithsonian
Institution, National Museum of American History, Kenneth
E. Behring Center.
All images supplied by Redferns Music Picture Library.
Edited and designed by D & N Publishing, Berkshire.
Printed and bound by Printing Express Ltd, Hong Kong.

09 08 07
3   2   1

Contents

Introduction 4

1   **Blues and roots** 12

2   **Swing and 'swing' and Satchmo** 30

3   **Bebop hard and cool** 72

4   **Freedom and fusion** 126

5   **In all languages** 160

Glossary 187

Need to know more? 190

Index 192

Introduction

As we move from the twentieth century – the jazz century – the music that has been called 'America's only art form' appears more multifaceted than ever. As a result, defining this now-venerable four-letter word is an ever more elusive enterprise, with any results destined to be as controversial as they have proven to be since the word jazz (or its early variant jass) first gained currency 90 years ago.

We surely cannot hope to return to the first jazz histories, written shortly before the Second World War, and find reliable guidance regarding what the music has become. Jazz has changed and – despite occasional creative troughs in which some have mourned its passing – is changing still.

So the language that we use to talk about jazz changes as well. The style that was originally played in New Orleans, which was jazz pure and simple during the 1920s (the 'Jazz Age'), became *traditional* jazz about 20 years later, to distinguish it from *modern* jazz. Someone should have foreseen the problems such a term invited, since it was not long before 'modern jazz' denoted a historically specific style of the music. Indeed, present-day jazz is no longer called modern (is present-day anything called modern?), and only the most commercially palatable style of today's jazz is called *contemporary*.

Yet the struggle to pin jazz down – to capture its essence – continues. The unabridged *Random House Dictionary of the English Language* touches the important bases in its primary definition, citing the music's origins around 1900 in New Orleans and its propulsive rhythms, stress on improvisation, and

> **did you know?**
>
> What's jazz? Fats Waller declared that if you have to ask, you'll never know.

An early photograph of jazz musicians in performance.

increasingly complex harmonies as time passed. Other definitions remind us that the term has also entered the popular vernacular as a synonym for excitement ('I'm all jazzed up') and excrement ('Don't give me any of that jazz'), without alluding to jazz's most notorious early usage as slang for sexual intercourse (as in 'The Jazz Me Blues'). This last, figuratively four-letter usage has struck some who create the music as so indicative of society's failure to honour both them and it that they have rejected the word *jazz* entirely.

Pianist Jimmy Rowles said that 'Jazz is a fleeting moment'.

Some practitioners have made their own attempts at definition. In an album title the pianist Jimmy Rowles called jazz a 'fleeting moment', complementing critic Whitney Balliet's more famous conceit that jazz is the sound of surprise. These notions stress the improvisational aspect of jazz, but does this mean that all jazz is improvisational? When Count Basie declared that jazz was nothing more than swinging the blues, did he mean all jazz? There was no mention of blues in the dictionary definition cited above, and Basie himself recorded loads of music

Pianist and bandleader Count Basie once offered that jazz is nothing more than 'swinging the blues'.

(including such signatures as 'April in Paris' and 'L'il Darlin'') that are not blues in structure or nuance. Basie's band always played with a propulsive rhythm, though, so is swing the essence we seek? Not unless we redefine that term to include the more irregular and esoteric rhythmic terrain of the free improvisers, the *clave* of Afro-Cuban music that informs Latin jazz, the samba inflections adapted from Brazilian bossa nova, and other international beats that jazz musicians hear and apply from around the world.

Today, the formats of certain radio stations have led some listeners to believe that any popular music without vocals, and in some cases any popular vocal music with a saxophone solo, is jazz. Many people who consider themselves jazz fans would argue that the music these stations play, often designated as *smooth jazz*, is really anti-jazz. That's the same basic position that some fans of the original New Orleans style adopted in the late 1930s when big bands became popular, or that many fans of the big bands took relating to bebop of the 1940s. And so it went in the early 1960s with the emergence of the avant-garde 'free' players and later in the decade when fusion appeared.

All of this should teach us, if not the need to abandon all standards, at least a bit of humility. To say that some viewed big bands as the smooth jazz of the Depression era is not to argue that Benny Goodman and Kenny G have equal value, though it should signal that the phrase 'jazz orthodoxy' has been and remains an oxymoron.

A more interesting question might be why so many different approaches have each been considered jazz at one time or another. There is something going

must know

The diverse musical styles that huddle under the descriptive umbrella *jazz* make it impossible to give a single, unqualified definition of this music.

The popularity of clarinetist Benny Goodman in the 1930s led to early debates about jazz as art versus jazz as entertainment.

on in this music, something beyond the conjunction of notes, that speaks to the way we live and the way we aspire to live. It has seeped into the way we talk and dress and the way we view the world. The progress of the music, from the fringes of respectable society to the pinnacles of current culture, suggests the magnitude of the change that this music has wrought. This is why the music's wider ramifications are an essential part of the jazz story and why two points that the dictionary definitions overlook must be kept in mind as we tell the jazz story.

Jazz is not just improvised, but in most cases also *collectively* improvised. Spontaneity alone would not distinguish jazz from, say, Mozart's piano concertos, which were originally performed with improvised cadenzas. Though unaccompanied solo performances have been created at all points in the jazz continuum, what really made jazz so audacious to its early audiences was the simultaneous invention heard when two or more musicians formed a jazz ensemble. The process is unmistakable in early performances such as those recorded by the King Oliver Creole Jazz Band, where cornets, clarinet and trombone spin variations collectively. Even after the individual soloist came to prominence in the recordings of Louis Armstrong's Hot Five and Hot

King Oliver's Creole Jazz Band, one of the first great jazz ensembles to be recorded. *Fourth from left*, **Oliver**; *second from right*, **Louis Armstrong**; *seated*, **Lil Hardin Armstrong**.

Seven, each player in the band maintained a certain leeway. Everyone is also improvising in the Charlie Parker Quintets of the 1940s and the Ornette Coleman Quartets of the 1960s; even the brass and reed sections of many big bands often worked without written arrangements and devised spontaneous background figures.

When a jazz group is inspired, each member makes maximum use of this creative freedom within the boundaries of his or her part in the ensemble, and as jazz has seen innovations arise, band members have found new ways to be free together. Mutual responsibility rather than anarchy is the result. The tenor saxophonist Joe Henderson said it as succinctly as possible when he titled one of his compositions and one of his albums *Our Thing*.

For Americans, there is another sense in which jazz is our thing. Many have claimed that, given its origins in the African American community and the predominance of African American innovators in its history, calling jazz American music gives too much credit to the majority culture. Yet drummer Art Blakey, one of the greatest and most African-inspired of the African American innovators, was fond of saying that he never heard indigenous music on his visits to Africa that met his definition of jazz. 'No America, no jazz' was something of a mantra for Blakey and indeed jazz may be the ultimate musical expression of the notion of America as melting pot. (This may also explain the tension between jazz as entertainment and jazz as art that is an ongoing theme in the music's history.)

This view is consistent with the frequently expressed notion that jazz is a musical manifestation of democracy, with each player in a

Ornette Coleman saw his music as 'the shape of jazz to come' in 1959.

must know

Give-and-take is so much a part of jazz performances that even the music's greatest individual geniuses haven't been able to succeed without sympathetic contributions from their supporting players.

Introduction

must know

In much of the world, jazz has come to symbolize America, and in societies ruled by forces of oppression it has been embraced as the sound-image of freedom.

band contributing an essential part that creates a whole greater than its individual components. As the trumpeter Wynton Marsalis has been heard to argue most prominently in recent years, jazz may be the product of American culture that comes closest to realizing the country's stated political ideals. Yet you do not have to be an American to play jazz. On the contrary, its enormous international appeal virtually from its inception has arguably made jazz the first and most inclusive example of 'world' music.

To best capture these interweaving themes and because jazz's evolution over the course of its history suggests that we score its development in scores of years, this book examines jazz in two-decade intervals. This approach is preferable to laying the basics out one instrument or one style at a time, while also giving emphasis to the various cometlike or extended careers of the major musicians that an alphabetical series of personal biographies can obscure. Jazz has not been a relay race, where one player or stylistic school rushes forward, only to halt after handing the evolutionary

Wynton Marsalis has argued that jazz is the ultimate realization of the American ideal.

baton to the next generation. It is more accurate to view jazz as a tree, with established stylistic branches continuing to proliferate even as new offshoots emerge and flourish.

Neither has jazz been driven by a constant trajectory of progress. It has seen peaks and valleys, surged and stayed in place, even looked backwards to reclaim missed opportunities. Jazz has also been inextricably tied to developments in technology, which have formed the historical archive by which we continue to reevaluate and revise the jazz story. Any number of musicians will argue that they, or those they revere, were never captured whole in recordings; yet recordings make it possible for us to continue to marvel at the genius of Louis Armstrong and Benny Goodman, Duke Ellington and Miles Davis and so many more.

But what if Fats Waller was correct and the need to enquire about jazz signals a basic lack of empathy? What if, as the cliché has it, you really do have to dig it to dig it? The alto saxophonist Julian 'Cannonball' Adderley may have been on to something when he remarked that being hip is a fact of life rather than a state of mind, since an analytical appreciation of jazz in the absence of a visceral response would be an incomplete appreciation indeed. Yet for many who find jazz intimidating, the problem may be more one of what you think you know, or perhaps what you think you don't know. Great jazz, like great literature, can operate on more than one level. To return to another term with multiple meanings, the more you dig (know), the more you can dig (appreciate). So, even if jazz has yet to become a fact of your life, please read on.

Julian 'Cannonball' Adderley suggested that an appreciation of jazz might be innate.

1 Blues and roots (jazz before 1920)

The spread of jazz in the first two decades of the twentieth century is astounding, given the technological limits of the time. On the basis of a few phonograph recordings, some piano rolls and the wanderlust of early jazz musicians, a style of music that was spawned primarily in black communities of the American South had spread across the country and begun to make inroads around the world. Jazz was already starting to signify freedom and forward thinking, and it would soon lend its name to a euphoric period that saw other musical styles redefined by its feeling and beat.

Roots and routes

There were no audio recordings of jazz before 1917, so we have to turn to other forms of evidence to discover how jazz took shape before 1920 – what we could call the music's prehistoric period.

must know

Jazz historians usually rely on sound recordings, but for the years prior to 1917 they have had to resort to other evidence, such as accounts passed down by those who heard the music firsthand.

Even after the startling success of the Original Dixieland Jazz Band's 'Livery Stable Blues' and 'Dixieland One-Step' – the first jazz 78 rpm recording and a million-seller upon its release in 1917 – recording companies remained more interested in classical artists and more polite dance orchestras.

The rolls of paper cut by seminal figures like Scott Joplin and Jelly Roll Morton for use in player pianos also provide only limited insight; they fail to capture nuances of touch and accent. Also, in a precursor to the overdubbing of later decades, piano rolls often contained added parts that made the resulting music almost impossible to play by a single pianist.

Morton and Joseph 'King' Oliver began to record in 1923, but jazz developed at such a rapid pace in this period that the music did not necessarily reflect what these and other artists sounded like 10 or 20 years earlier. Many witnesses who lived in New Orleans and were familiar with the music played there during the 1897–1917 heyday of the city's infamous Storyville district insisted that the first recordings by Oliver's Creole Jazz Band represent a significant evolution from his earlier style. Some even swore that the real sounds of Storyville were never captured on recordings.

In the soundbite version of jazz's origins, rhythmic African music and harmonic European

Jelly Roll Morton left piano rolls that offer suggestions of how early jazz sounded.

Cornetist Joe 'King' Oliver was one of the first jazz pioneers to record his music – but not until 1923.

composition merge in the black and Creole neighborhoods of New Orleans, taking root there and then migrating north and east by riverboat just prior to the 1920s. But this capsule creation myth glosses over a far more complex and widespread history. When Morton, Oliver and their peers began to develop what the world came to know as jazz, they were able to draw upon nearly a century of African-influenced musical styles developed all over America and the Caribbean. And many of these innovators didn't wait for the shutdown of New Orleans's red light district, or the next paddle wheeler leaving from the local port, to take what they had learned on the road.

Africa

Africa was an essential source point for jazz music, inspiring such key jazz elements as rhythmic expression, improvisation, call-and-response and narrative techniques, and interactive spirituality.

did you know?

The banjo, a prominent instrument during jazz's early years, originated in Africa.

Africa fed jazz with rhythmic and formal inspirations, and even with an instrument in the case of the banjo.

In Africa, unlike Europe, rhythm served as the primary element of musical expression, and ensembles composed entirely of percussion instruments created extended polyrhythmic works. African music was not committed to paper; it was an oral (or more accurately an aural) tradition, learned by ear and therefore more naturally subject to spontaneous variation. Techniques such as call-and-response patterns, where a lead voice is answered by the surrounding ensemble, and narrative forms such as the insult-laden songs of allusion from West Africa would reappear as central components of the jazz style.

Religious music

The power of African musical ideas was felt in the Western Hemisphere long before 1900, and far beyond the confines of a single community. Africa influenced evolving styles of religious music, at first through the survival of *vodun* (voodoo) societies in Catholic portions of the New World, where European religious practices were less likely to be imposed upon the slaves than in the Protestant American South. This gave African religious music a foothold in New Orleans, where the slaves were allowed to dance and play instruments in Congo Square beginning in 1817, as well as in Cuba and Haiti.

Traces of African influence were also entering Christian religious practice. Camp meetings and revivals, popular in rural and frontier America during much of the nineteenth century, frequently featured black preachers who preached in a florid, interactive style that was at times similar to the trancelike states of the *vodun* societies and anticipated the congregational fervour of later gospel services.

A more formal merger of African and European musical influences led to circle dances or 'ring shouts', which were first described in the Civil War period. In these musical expressions, improvised variations on short, rhythmic melodies (later called 'blue notes') were created through call-and-response patterns. Concert performances of Negro spirituals, which became popular after the first tour of the Fisk Jubilee Singers in 1871, are another example of the African/European synthesis.

Minstrel shows

American secular music was also showing the influence of Africa in a variety of ways. During the last half of the nineteenth century, minstrel shows were the most popular form of entertainment throughout the country. They presented a caricature of Negro life that lingered until the civil rights era of the 1960s. Minstrel shows mixed dramatic vignettes and vaudeville acts performed by Caucasians in blackface like the popular Thomas D. 'Daddy Jim Crow' Rice. They featured stylizations of black music by white composers like Stephen Foster. The shows were a two-edged sword, stereotyping and stigmatizing the manners of the former slaves while also spreading their culture and subtly mocking the mainstream.

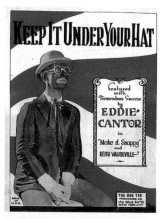

The influence of nineteenth-century minstrelsy and spiritual singing resonated into the following century.

did you know?

The cakewalk, a popular dance craze that formed the centerpiece of many minstrel shows, originated on plantations in the American South with slaves who mocked their masters' behaviour.

Ragtime and blues

As more sophisticated, spontaneous – even revolutionary – styles of African American music arose, minstrel shows helped disseminate them to audiences around the country. Two such styles, which we can consider jazz's siblings rather than its strict chronological precursors, were ragtime and blues.

did you know?

When Jelly Roll Morton made his invaluable Library of Congress recordings in 1938, he used Joplin's 'Maple Leaf Rag' to illustrate how ragtime had generated – and then been superceded by – the new jazz approach.

Scott Joplin's ragtime compositions for solo piano created a phenomenon at the beginning of the twentieth century.

Ragtime

Ragtime was initially a midwestern phenomenon. The style initially became identified with St Louis, Missouri, where Scott Joplin and other itinerant pianists gained initial fame near the turn of the century, and it quickly turned into a popular fad with the rise of the cakewalk. The music is totally composed, with distinct sections usually of 16 bars that suggest a classical rondo. But ragtime's defining characteristic is its staggered, ragged, syncopated melodies that place accents on unexpected beats and create a momentum anticipating what we now call 'swing'. Popular entertainers and songwriters, including the composer Irving Berlin, who wrote the hit song 'Alexander's Ragtime Band' in 1911, quickly embraced the dramatic tension in such ragtime classics as Joplin's 'Maple Leaf Rag' of 1899, with the pendulum steadiness of the left-hand figures working against the more unpredictable right-hand accents.

At the same time, ragtime was making an impression on pianists more inclined to depart from the music's written scores and embellish performances with their own spontaneous variations. Pianists Luckey Roberts, Willie 'The Lion' Smith and James P. Johnson had begun to work their looser and more ornate variations on ragtime into what would be called 'rent party' or 'stride piano' before anything called 'jazz' had formally arrived in New York. And in New Orleans, Tony Jackson, Jelly Roll Morton and other pianists were playing with the forms, rhythms and breaks of ragtime in search of a more spontaneous approach.

The blues

Both spirituals and ragtime compositions formed essential components in the repertoire of early jazz bands and jazz soloists. Given the secular and informal nature of America, though, it was unlikely that either sacred songs or rigorously notated piano scores could launch a revolutionary musical language. That role fell to the blues, a subject as rich at its core and hazy at its boundaries as jazz itself. Laments about oppressive living and working conditions provided early blues texts, though what we think of as the blues quickly took on more romantic subject matter that encompassed defiance and determination as well as the sorrow indicated when someone admits to 'having the blues'.

Pianist Willie 'The Lion' Smith, an early master of stride piano, with his trademark cigar but minus his equally familiar derby.

Many itinerant and undocumented blues singers disseminated what would become a basic form of jazz and other African American music.

The early years of the twentieth century saw the spread of what would become the blues' most common and profound structure, a form both compact in its contours and inexhaustible in its implications. The twelve-bar, AAB blues presents a grid more compact than the sonnet yet potentially as vast as the epic. An initial four-bar stanza is first repeated and then resolved. There are basic modulations to the subdominant chord at bar five and the dominant chord at bar nine. The flatted third and seventh scale tones in a chord lend a

must know

The blues dates back to the work songs of plantation slaves, which carried over to the cries of itinerant street vendors at the turn of the century.

did you know?

Gertrude 'Ma' Rainey first heard the blues in 1902 when she was 16. Two years later she was singing them in a minstrel show – and was soon billed as the 'Mother of the Blues'.

W. C. Handy collected and published early blues songs, leaving the true paternity of the style in question.

must know

W. C. Handy earned the title 'Father of the Blues', but the true authorship of some of his songs is debatable.

distinctive feeling. Musicologists tell us that even the harmonic characteristics can be traced back to Africa rather than Europe, making the blues one of the purest products of the African American experience.

While the earliest blues were performed by itinerant singers who accompanied themselves on guitar or piano, entertainers working in the more commercialized minstrel and vaudeville shows quickly picked up the style. W. C. Handy was a cornetist and bandleader who had already performed in minstrel show bands and vocal quartets when, in 1903, he heard a slide guitarist play and sing 'The Yellow Dog Blues' in Tutwiler, Mississippi. This inspired Handy to collect additional examples of the new song form, and ultimately to copyright his discoveries as original compositions.

The 'father' of the blues

It is beyond dispute, however, that Handy's 'Memphis Blues', a 1912 reworking of the political campaign song 'Mr. Crump' that he penned three years earlier, was the first published blues. Two years later 'St Louis Blues' was an even bigger success and became the epitome of the genre. Dance orchestras were recording Handy's compositions before the Original Dixieland Jazz Band (ODJB) made its first record, but it was the ODJB's success that provided the opportunity for Handy's Orchestra of Memphis to make its own recordings in 1917, including several blues as well as two rags. The stiff results indicate that Handy's primary talent was as a composer or, less charitably, a compiler.

New Orleans

All of this music – spirituals, minstrel songs, ragtime, blues and the rest – came together in the incredible cauldron that was early twentieth-century New Orleans. This port city near the mouth of the Mississippi River with its distinctive French/Creole background had always been more open to the African traditions of slaves than other American urban centres, and shortly after the Civil War it witnessed a blossoming of music.

The newly freed blacks formed fraternal organizations and other, often secret societies reflecting *vodun* traditions. These societies featured orchestras that incorporated a variety of music, including the popular marches played by French military bands. When a member of the society died, the orchestra would perform at the funerals and wakes, marching to and from the cemetery and attracting a 'second line' of celebrants that harkened back to burial traditions in Dahomey. These bands were also heard on less solemn occasions, including the picnics and dances that were central to the black community's social life.

did you know?

The term 'jazz' was first applied to Brown's Dixieland Jass Band, during a Chicago appearance in 1915.

New Orleans brass bands on their way to a cemetery, with second-liners in the background prepared for the celebratory return trip.

Creoles of Color

Representing a mixture of Spanish, French and African ancestry, the Creoles were a distinctive caste in the early years of Reconstruction, clearly treated as inferior to Caucasians yet holding themselves above the Negroes. Creole families nurtured their European roots and frequently provided their children with training in European music. It was a shock to the Creoles, once the white reaction to Reconstruction set in, to find that the white majority considered them an undifferentiated part of the coloured underclass. Creoles saw blacks as ignorant and unrefined, while black musicians tended to find Creoles technically proficient but lacking in emotional and creative depth. Prejudice was not simply expressed in terms of pure black and pure white.

Storyville spreads the message

The white majority was exposed to the music of the black orchestras and the Creole musicians as well, especially after Storyville was established as an officially sanctioned centre for gambling parlours, houses of prostitution and other 'sporting' establishments. In its 20 years of existence, this precursor to today's adult entertainment zones was a hotbed of what would become jazz. Storyville establishments provided the employment that allowed many who otherwise had to subsist on manual labour to become professional musicians, and had much to do with creating the aura of disrepute that was initially attached to jazz, and with enhancing its sexual connotations. Storyville also gave members of the ODJB and other white New Orleans musicians direct exposure to this radical new music.

New Orleans, Louisiana, as it looked at the time of jazz music's infancy.

The first jazz legend

Jazz's first legend, cornetist Charles 'Buddy' Bolden and his Ragtime Band, dominated music in New Orleans for the first decade of Storyville's existence. Though his life ended in tragedy, his influence was lasting.

A cylinder recording said to be made by Bolden's group around the time of Storyville's inception has never surfaced, so we know Bolden by one surviving photograph and stories of his romantic and business exploits. These stories have proved to be as unsound as the notion that his horn could be heard for several miles. What Bolden (born in 1868) does appear to have possessed was a solid grounding in brass band and church music and an ear for every other variety of sound being played at the end of the nineteenth century.

The only known photograph of New Orleans' first trumpet king, Buddy Bolden, who holds a cornet and stands next to the bassist.

Bolden's band

The band that Buddy Bolden formed in the 1890s is definitive of what the world would come to know as the traditional New Orleans jazz ensemble. Bolden's lead part was complemented by the more liquid high lines of a clarinet and the pungent lower flourishes of a valve horn or trombone. The rough polyphony of the band's intersecting lines teased and tugged the borders of the marches and rags in its repertoire. Known as 'King' Buddy at his peak, Bolden possessed a fragile temperament that grew more erratic with his increased consumption of alcohol. An arrest during the 1906 Labor Day parade preceded Bolden's commitment a year later to a mental institution.

did you know?

Jazz legend William Geary 'Bunk' Johnson, who played in the Bolden band as a teenager, wasn't recorded until 1942.

Freddie Keppard, one pioneer who guarded his secrets for fear of being copied.

did you know?

The Oliver/Ory ensembles were the ultimate expression of New Orleans ensemble music in its native environment. They included clarinetists Sidney Bechet and Johnny Dodds, and eventually the teenage cornetist Louis Armstrong.

He remained there, undocumented save as jazz's first tragic figure, until his death in 1931.

Bolden's influence

Fortunately, Buddy Bolden's message had been heard by a younger generation of New Orleans brass men, none of whom surpassed the King's reputation for charisma or sheer power, but who did keep their wits about them longer and survived to be documented on record. One was Freddie Keppard, who assumed the leadership of the already successful Olympia Orchestra in 1906 at age 16. He later played in such fabled outfits as the Original Creole Band and the Eagle Band, and his sound and phrasing were said to be closest to Bolden's. Keppard introduced muted effects with water glasses and beer bottles in the bell of his cornet, as well as fingering techniques that he concealed from his rivals by draping a handkerchief over his horn. A fear of being plagiarized led Keppard to turn down an opportunity to record shortly before the ODJB was first documented. The recordings Keppard did make in the 1920s showed the effects of his own drinking problem.

Joe Oliver, however, inherited Bolden's crown and became a primary early ambassador of New Orleans music. According to legend, he became King Oliver in 1910 at the age of 25 by standing on a Storyville street where Keppard was performing and blowing a blues with a strength and purity that Keppard could not match. Whether the story is true or apocryphal, Oliver soon had Keppard's job at Pete Lala's Café, where he led bands or worked in the group of trombonist Edward 'Kid' Ory for several years.

Jelly Roll Morton

In the parlours of such Storyville haunts as Lulu White's and Tom Anderson's Annex, pianists rivaled bands for prominence. The dominant pianist historically, thanks in part to his own talent for self-promotion, is Ferdinand Joseph LaMonthe, better known to the world as Jelly Roll Morton.

As adept at hustling pool and fabricating a biography as he was at playing and writing music, Morton made numerous claims that have not survived historical research. His declaration, in a 1938 letter to *Down Beat*, that he 'created' jazz in 1902 grows even more fantastic now that scholars have determined that Morton was all of twelve years old at the time. Yet the sense of outrage that prompted Morton to write to the magazine, and to dismiss such pretenders to innovation in his eyes as W. C. Handy and the ODJB, was rooted in honest achievement.

Morton was a master of fusion decades before the term gained musical meaning. He brought together

Jelly Roll Morton in performance (*above*), and giving instruction to one of his Red Hot Peppers recording units (*left*).

Unlike other early New Orleans players, Kid Ory eschewed a trip up the Mississippi River in favour of the West Coast.

the syncopated motion and contrasting structure of ragtime, the more rolling beat of the pianoless marching bands, and the dipping *habanera* rhythms of Latin music. Even styles he held in low regard, like the blues (which, as a Creole, he considered a crude and limited form), became ingredients in the speciality numbers he performed in the brothels while still a teenager. Morton, like Handy, undoubtedly put his name to more than one melody that was in the public domain. But Morton had a genius for shaping and strengthening such raw materials with rhythmic contrast, dramatic breaks and transitional passages that were later developed from his piano solos into full band arrangements.

The music hits the road

While Morton's New Orleans period, like Oliver's, did not survive on recordings, both men had a major impact outside their native city long before their first visit to a studio. Morton travelled to other southern states before 1910, appeared in New York's Harlem in 1911 (where James P. Johnson, soon to be the leading exponent of stride piano, heard him play the blues) and was working throughout California and Mexico between 1915 and 1923.

Similarly, African Americans, seeking better employment opportunities and escape from the more oppressive forms of segregation, streamed out of the South in the early decades of the century, and their music inevitably followed. Freddie Keppard visited both coasts with the touring Original Creole Band before settling in Chicago in 1918, while Keppard's rival Joe Oliver also visited Chicago a year later, the same year in which Kid Ory became a California resident.

The Original Dixieland Jazz Band

As the 1920s approached, both white and black musicians were travelling to Chicago, New York and beyond, eventually reaching Europe. Through live performances and the first jazz recordings, they successfully spread the uninhibited New Orleans style to national and international audiences.

One group of white musicians, Brown's Dixieland Band, labelled a 'jass' band as a slur by the Chicago musicians' union in 1915, was said to reflect more of the minstrel tradition, with novelty effects and other kinds of 'hokum' predominating. Brown's band did familiarize the public with the term *jass*, however, and revealed the growing national interest in the new music style.

A year later, again in Chicago, another group of white New Orleanians took shape and used the term in their name – the Original Dixieland Jass Band. But band members paid more attention to black players like King Oliver, and the front line of cornetist Nick LaRocca, trombonist Eddie Edwards and clarinetist Larry Shields was a direct expression of the Bolden legacy. The ODJB's Chicago success led to a job offer in New York, where it opened at Reisenweber's Café on 26 January 1917, and became an immediate sensation.

The first jazz recording

Columbia Records documented the band two weeks later, then found the results to be in such questionable taste that the music was not immediately issued. The Victor label, having fewer compunctions, recorded the ODJB shortly thereafter and quickly released the results. With hindsight, we can hear the limitations of the ODJB members as soloists, the crudity of their arrangements and their reliance on barnyard effects. We can also dismiss the band's early notoriety as fountainheads of

James Reese Europe gave early hints of how jazz would sound in an orchestral context.

jazz as the first instance of black innovations appropriated by and credited to white imitators. Once the war ended, the ODJB visited Europe, where LaRocca, as avid a self-promoter as Morton, declared that the band represented musical anarchy.

The prehistoric big band

The instant impact of the ODJB can be seen in the career of James Reese Europe, the most successful African American bandleader in New York at the time. Europe rose to fame accompanying the white dance team of Vernon and Irene Castle, and his 1913–1914 recordings (issued under the name of Europe's Society Orchestra) were the first by a black bandleader. While strongly syncopated, these performances were not jazz. After enlisting in the war effort, however, Europe organized an all-black band called the Hell Fighters that was advertised as a jazz band when it toured the continent. Recordings made shortly before Europe was murdered in 1919, including versions of Handy's most popular blues and the ODJB's 'Clarinet Marmalade', contain the breaks characteristic of early jazz and a stronger rhythmic character than other military bands possessed. This was orchestral dance music taking its first steps towards the liberation of swing, but it had a long way to go.

Jazz goes international

Beyond the aesthetic achievements of the Hell Fighters, the band had great success touring the European continent during the war. Other orchestras soon crossed the Atlantic, including Will Marion Cook's Southern Syncopated Orchestra, which featured the New Orleans clarinetist Sidney Bechet. Ernst Ansermet, the Swiss conductor who had premiered Stravinsky's 'Rite of Spring', was overwhelmed when he heard Bechet. In a 1919 review that is considered the first important piece of jazz criticism, Ansermet proclaimed that Bechet was 'the first of his race to have composed perfectly formed blues on the clarinet' and predicted that Bechet's approach was 'the highway the whole world will swing along tomorrow'.

Ansermet had that last part right, although the musician who paved that highway was a contemporary of Bechet's who was still working in New Orleans.

Sidney Bechet was the subject of the first piece of serious jazz criticism.

must know

The Hell Fighters' success was the first indication that jazz, or at least music on its way to becoming jazz, could become a musical international language.

want to know more?

The songs listed below, along with the musicians or groups who performed them, are some of the highlights of the era.
- W. C. Handy
  'Memphis Blues'
  'St Louis Blues'
- Scott Joplin
  'Maple Leaf Rag'
- Original Dixieland Jazz Band
  'At the Jazz Band Ball'
  'Clarinet Marmalade'
  'Dixieland One-Step'
  'Livery Stable Blues'
  'Tiger Rag'
- James Reese Europe
  'Jazz Baby'

2 Swing and 'swing' and Satchmo (1921–1940)

Despite the premium it places on collective improvisation, jazz, like any other music, has depended upon the example of great individuals. For a new style to be completely expressed, all members of an ensemble need to be able to play in a common rhythmic and harmonic language. Likewise, new ideas exchanged between like-minded artists have been invaluable as jazz has evolved. But at critical moments in jazz history, the single voice of genius has been commanding enough to bring all other voices forwards.

Louis Armstrong, seminal figure

In these years jazz came into its own, growing more diverse and sophisticated, leaving its mark in other areas of music and culture. One man is primarily responsible for this change, and his impact was as far-reaching and profound as that of any other twentieth-century musician.

Louis Armstrong soon became a familiar figure worldwide.

His name is Louis Armstrong. It is indicative of his importance to both his country and his era that, despite proof that his actual date of birth was 4 August 1901, his claim to have been born on 4 July 1900 continues to carry a poetic veracity that overshadows the hard facts of baptism certificates and census records.

Armstrong is New Orleans's number one son, and his musical career began in a vocal quartet on the city's street corners before he was a teenager. After firing off blanks from his stepfather's revolver during the 1913 New Year's celebrations, Armstrong was committed to the Colored Waif's Home for Boys, a sentence that allowed him to learn the cornet and perform in an orchestra.

did you know?

Louis Armstrong showed obvious musical talent even as a teenager. When Joe 'King' Oliver left Kid Ory's band, Ory chose the young Armstrong as Oliver's replacement.

Leaving home, heading north

Armstrong would soon take to the road, playing in the riverboat orchestra of pianist Fate Marable on excursions that took the youngster and other important New Orleans musicians to the northern extremes of the Mississippi River well before their music was documented on record. After completing a cruise with Marable, Armstrong always returned home until his idol King Oliver, now leader of the

successful Creole Jazz Band at Chicago's Lincoln Gardens Café, brought him north to play second cornet in the summer of 1922.

One of pianist Fate Marable's riverboat ensembles that spread the New Orleans style up and down the Mississippi River.

The Creole Jazz Band records

The historic recordings that Oliver's band made the following year at a Richmond, Indiana, studio and in Chicago remain powerful statements despite the severe limitations of the acoustical recording process for early 78 rpm records. Individual parts often merge in the polyphonic blend of two cornets, clarinet (Johnny Dodds), trombone (most often Honore Dutrey) and rhythm (including pianist Lil Hardin and drummer Warren 'Baby' Dodds), but the musicians' syncopated strength, emotional force and absence of hokum place Oliver's band far beyond the ODJB. The tracks 'Chimes Blues', 'Tears' and 'Snake Rag' also feature Armstrong's rhythmic sophistication and melodic clarity in solos, lead passages and two-cornet breaks executed with Oliver.

did you know?

Lillian Hardin, pianist in the Creole Jazz Band, married Louis Armstrong in 1924.

Jimmy McPartland and other young Chicagoans were among the first white musicians to fall under the spell of jazz.

The first disciples – the Austin High Gang

Oliver's records, as well as an even earlier series of Gennetts by the greatest of the white New Orleans ensembles, the New Orleans Rhythm Kings (NORK), document a music that was turning the heads of an entire generation of white teenage musicians in Chicago. While these new sounds attracted youngsters from all parts of the city, many of the most talented and committed attended Austin High School, and as a group they became known as the Austin High Gang. Such important players of the future as trumpeters Jimmy McPartland and Francis 'Muggsy' Spanier, clarinetist Benny Goodman, tenor saxophonist Lawrence 'Bud' Freeman, banjo player/guitarist Eddie Condon and drummers Gene Krupa and George Wettling would gather in ice cream parlours to play records, stand outside dancehalls and speakeasies that they were too young to enter, or, if they were lucky, sneak into the dark corners of these establishments to hear the new sounds.

Chicago, the jazz mecca

Soon other white youngsters were arriving in Chicago with jazz on their mind, including cornetist Leon 'Bix' Beiderbecke from Davenport, Iowa, who had first heard Armstrong during one of Fate Marable's visits. The Friars' Inn and the music played there by the NORK made the earliest impressions, but King Oliver and his young second trumpeter quickly became the favourites. Several of the Austin High Gang began to bring their instruments to the Lincoln Gardens and acquire firsthand experience when Oliver invited them to sit in.

Armstrong and Henderson

Armstrong's influence would not be confined to Chicago for long. Once he reached New York, his circle expanded to include stints working with such jazz greats as Fletcher Henderson, Don Redman, Coleman Hawkins, Sidney Bechet and Bessie Smith.

Armstrong continued to act as a magnet for aspiring musicians when he left Oliver in 1924 and began working under his own name across the street from Lincoln Gardens at the Sunset Café.

At the urging of Lil, his confident and ambitious new bride, Armstrong soon accepted an offer to join Fletcher Henderson's orchestra in New York. Henderson had formed his first band in 1921 to accompany singer Ethel Waters on her national tour of black theatres. While in New Orleans on this tour, Henderson first heard Armstrong and offered him a job. Armstrong turned that chance down because there was no room in Henderson's band for drummer and Armstrong friend Zutty Singleton. This was a rare recruiting failure for Henderson, who already was

> **did you know?**
> Fletcher Henderson was a college-educated black southerner who pursued a career in music when he couldn't earn a living using his training in chemistry. A competent pianist, Henderson became one of big band's leading arrangers.

Fletcher Henderson, sitting behind the bass drum for this photo, was in fact a pianist and the leader of jazz's first great big band. He already had two star soloists in this 1924 photo – tenor saxophonist Coleman Hawkins (*on floor at left*) and Louis Armstrong (*seated, second from left*).

Coleman Hawkins paid close attention to Armstrong and, in the process, became acknowledged as the father of the jazz saxophone.

gaining a reputation for obtaining the services of the best musicians.

By the time Armstrong decided to join Henderson's band, two other seminal figures were already aboard: Don Redman and Coleman Hawkins. Alto saxophonist Redman was responsible for the best of the band's early arrangements, and for the discrete use of trumpet, trombone and reed sections that amplified the usual approach of a three-horn New Orleans ensemble. Tenor saxophonist Hawkins was already hailed as a technical wizard specializing in an aggressive slap-tongue technique. Despite the obvious technical strengths of these and other musicians in the band, early Henderson recordings sound stiff and unauthentic, with a rote approach to the dance tunes performed at the band's regular Roseland Ballroom job and contrived effects on the occasional stomp or blues title. This changed quickly once Armstrong began recording with Henderson in the autumn of 1924.

Armstrong's impact

What Armstrong brought to Henderson over the next 14 months, clearly audible in such recordings as 'Go 'Long Mule', 'Copenhagen' and 'Everybody Loves My Baby', was a new way to allow the music to breathe that was instantly infectious. The herky-jerky, uninflected rhythms in Redman's modifications of stock dance band arrangements and the blustery Hawkins approach to the saxophone gave way to flowing, vibrant tempos and melodically shapely and blues-drenched improvised lines – the very qualities that made Armstrong's solos and lead lines so memorable. These discoveries were revelations to talented musicians like Redman and especially Hawkins, whose own advanced harmonic ideas and virtuoso execution provided the model for chord-based improvising (or 'playing the changes') that would blossom over the decade that Hawkins spent as Henderson's star soloist.

The first great big band

Henderson developed Armstrong's rhythmic and melodic ideas in the context of Redman's sectionalized, riff-based arranging style. When Redman left in 1927, Henderson became more active as an arranger, while also calling upon his brother Horace and the young multi-instrumentalist Benny Carter (particularly adept at scoring saxophone ensembles) for important contributions. In Henderson's hands, music with a New Orleans pedigree, including 'Sugarfoot Stomp' and Jelly Roll Morton's 'King Porter Stomp', became frequently recorded signature tunes. The former was a retitling of King Oliver's 'Dippermouth Blues', with Oliver's famous three-chorus solo played verbatim. 'I'm Coming Virginia', 'Somebody Loves Me' and other popular songs also acquired a jazz flavour. A parade of striking soloists, including Rex Stewart (cornet), Henry 'Red' Allen (trumpet), Jimmy Harrison (trombone) and William 'Buster' Bailey (clarinet), joined the reliable Hawkins.

Armstrong and the blues singers

During his time in New York with Henderson, Armstrong found more extensive opportunities to expose his trumpet on a series of small-group recordings, many of which found him accompanying blues singers. These sessions might be considered the initial evidence that jazz was about to become a soloist's medium, with individual musicians who commanded sufficient virtuosity and imagination to build and sustain lengthy improvisations outside the

must know

Fletcher Henderson created the blueprint for the tightly arranged and star-laden jazz orchestra – and for what would become known as big band swing. He did it using many of Louis Armstrong's techniques.

polyphonic context popularized by Oliver and the NORK. These recordings also indicated how inexhaustible the blues form would prove to be in the hands of inspired interpreters.

Perhaps the only two performers capable of operating at Armstrong's level in this period shared the spotlight on several of these recordings. Sidney Bechet, now concentrating on a soprano saxophone he had purchased in London, proved equally capable of dominating an ensemble on recordings released under the name of Clarence Williams' Blue Five and the Red Onion Jazz Babies. Bessie Smith, acknowledged as the Empress of the Blues, never sounded more commanding than on the nine tracks she recorded with Armstrong in support during 1925.

Blues singers played a key role in disseminating jazz, none more so than Bessie Smith.

The Hot Five and Hot Seven

Armstrong returned to Chicago in 1925. His impact soon widened through ground-breaking ensemble recordings that showcased individual artists, and his own personal appearances as a featured soloist with other orchestras.

What ultimately turned small-group jazz away from the polyphonic New Orleans ensemble and towards individual voices was the series of recordings Armstrong made under his own name for the OKeh label after he returned to Chicago. The featured ensembles still looked like Oliver's band and even included several of the same musicians, but the orientation was far more streamlined.

Louis Armstrong's Hot Five and Hot Seven played music arranged to feature the performers in individual solos. If the format revealed limitations of technique and invention in such older participants as Ory and Johnny Dodds, they elevated Armstrong, a musician who

must know

The switch from acoustical to electric recording made it possible to more accurately capture the sounds of tuba and drums.

Louis Armstrong's Hot Five, 1925 edition, with (*from left*) Armstrong, Johnny St Cyr, Johnny Dodds, Kid Ory and Lil Hardin.

seemed to know no limits. His choruses dart and flow, his breaks crackle, as rippling glissandi and precisely placed high notes keep company with harmonic notions that look to the future. Rhythmically, Armstrong was even more daring, pushing and pulling against the more flowing 4/4 tempo implied by his solos, adding the gliding release of relaxation that was the necessary complement to earlier jazz's ragged tensions.

Earl 'Fatha' Hines, whose innovative concepts and partnership with Armstrong led commentators to describe his approach as 'trumpet-style' piano.

Classic recordings

Several titles Armstrong recorded during this period became instant classics, including 'Cornet Chop Suey', 'Big Butter and Egg Man', 'Wild Man Blues', 'Potato Head Blues' and 'Struttin' with Some Barbecue'. No Armstrong records, in this period or later, surpass two 1928 interpretations of Oliver compositions. 'West End Blues', featuring a late version of the Hot Five, summarizes the range and complexity of Armstrong's art – an abstract and mercurial opening cadenza, straightforward and emotionally charged theme statement and dramatic valedictory chorus in which a single sustained note explodes into whorls of energy. The duet 'Weather Bird' is a seamless abstraction of ragtime structure, displaying the limits to which improvisers could stretch established forms. Both performances also showcase Pittsburgh native Earl 'Fatha' Hines, whose exposure to Armstrong in Chicago led him to develop a similar linear fluency in his own solos. The connection was so strong that Hines became known for playing the piano 'trumpet style', a tribute to the melodic clarity of his right hand.

The working reality

The great irony surrounding the Hot Five and Hot Seven recordings is that they in no way represent the music Armstrong played as a working musician. As Chicago's boldest and most charismatic soloist, he was in great demand for featured spots with the orchestras that performed in the city's theatres and ballrooms. These were not jazz bands per se, but popular ensembles that played the hit songs of the day as well as light classical material, and accompanied featured singers, dancers and comedians. One band that employed Armstrong, Erskine Tate's Vendome Orchestra, played at the Vendome cinema, and provided accompaniment to silent films as well as stage show interludes, and where Armstrong took a featured turn along with several speciality acts.

After the final screening, Armstrong would finish the night at the Sunset Café with another orchestra led by Carroll Dickerson. Some of the speakeasies and nightclubs featured combos, with Johnny Dodds leading the small band at Kelly's Stables and Hines working at the Apex Club with another of New Orleans' finest clarinetists, Jimmie Noone; yet even many of the clubs had switched to larger bands and floorshows by the late 1920s, and musicians who might blow informally at speakeasies on week-nights hoped to land more lucrative society and ballroom work on weekends. The Roaring Twenties image of Chicago jazz, with bootleggers like Al Capone arriving in clubs, locking the doors and then tipping band members generously as his requests were answered, was real enough, although by 1930 such scenes were more likely to take place in a ballroom such as the Grand Terrace, where Hines now led an orchestra.

> **must know**
>
> Armstrong's Hot Five and Hot Seven recordings are as influential a series as any in jazz history.

The growth of jazz recording

Record companies realized that a public already existed for this new music. It was rooted in the southern black communities where the music first took shape and in the black neighbourhoods of northern cities that had been created by the Great Migration. But those roots were also expanding to other sectors of society through the contributions of white musicians such as bandleader Paul Whiteman and cornetist Bix Beiderbecke.

Mamie Smith, the first if not the best of the singers who popularized blues' vocals in the 1920s.

Race records, as they were already labelled and would continue to be known for another two decades, had produced commercial successes since Mamie Smith released the first hit blues vocal, 'Crazy Blues', in 1920. Race records featured raw sounds and lyrics as well as a good share of salty humour, at a time when the newfangled phenomena blues and jazz were still considered out-of-bounds in polite society. In many instances the material was simplified for audiences that were presumed incapable of appreciating such fare as the 'Poet and Peasant Overture', which Armstrong was performing nightly with Erskine Tate.

Paul Whiteman

As Armstrong's recordings gained influence, and as new companies entered the recording industry, other black musicians who worked in orchestras found opportunities to record in intimate surroundings. So did many white musicians, who found their working environment even more restrictive. Despite the inroads that jazz was making among white bandleaders, even the hugely successful Paul Whiteman, the man portrayed as the King of Jazz in a film of the period, only used jazz as one flavour in a mix that also included ballads, novelty songs and light classics.

The musicians that Whiteman and his competitors began hiring to play occasional solo choruses and breaks, and who otherwise worked even more anonymously in studio orchestras, also grew hungry for creative outlets. The best of them, including cornetist Ernest 'Red' Nichols, trombonists Irving 'Miff' Mole and Tommy Dorsey and saxophonist Jimmy Dorsey, also began to organize small recording units in New York, often under fanciful names like the Charleston Chasers and the Red Heads.

White jazz in the 1920s

These early examples of white jazz featured smoother ensemble work than recordings made by either the New Orleans pioneers or Chicago's Austin High

Popular bandleader Paul Whiteman incorporated jazz techniques and a few great jazz soloists into his popular orchestra.

Joe Venuti's chosen instrument, the violin, was heard in early 'chamber jazz' recordings.

Leon 'Bix' Beiderbecke, among jazz's first great soloists and tragic figures.

disciples, with a frequent emphasis on instruments other than horns (Joe Venuti's violin, Eddie Lang's guitar, Kenneth 'Red' Norvo's xylophone), suggesting hot chamber music. The absence of a dominant personality such as Armstrong on some of these performances lent a greater overall balance to the resulting music, although one player did emerge who became a creative focal point. He played a cornet, as Armstrong initially had, and during his far shorter life he exerted a similar fascination.

Bix Beiderbecke

Bix Beiderbecke died a burnt-out alcoholic in 1931, at the age of 28, and the details of his life, as embellished in the 1938 Dorothy Baker novel *Young Man with a Horn*, came to epitomize the fate of the Jazz Age rebel to an extent exceeded only by F. Scott Fitzgerald's tale of Jay Gatsby. An Iowa native from a prosperous family, Beiderbecke was a brilliant but untrained musician who heard New Orleans music on the riverboats that visited his home town of Davenport. After making early Gennett recordings with the Wolverines, he sat in with Oliver and Armstrong in Chicago. Work in the Midwest with saxophonist Frankie Trumbauer and bandleader Jean Goldkette followed, then more small-group recordings in 1927 issued primarily under Trumbauer's name. Beiderbecke also recorded an original composition on piano, 'In a Mist', that employed harmonies commonly associated with contemporary European composers.

Beiderbecke proved to be the perfect tragic icon, a raw genius who stunned his fellow musicians in one-shot recording situations yet aspired to create symphonies, and who drank himself to death out of frustration and lack of recognition. No doubt he was exposed to musical possibilities far different from those confronting Armstrong and the other black musical pioneers whom Beiderbecke admired, but we remember him not because he transcended jazz but because he brought other possibilities within the music's orbit.

Beiderbecke's legacy

With his pure sound and knack for sustaining melodic invention, and in his more settled yet still surprising use of rhythm, Beiderbecke demonstrated that jazz could encompass profound personal expression not drawn directly from African American experience. Black musicians including Armstrong and Rex Stewart, one of Armstrong's successors in the Henderson band, paid attention to Beiderbecke not because he sounded black but because he drew from the common pool of jazz techniques in order to sound like himself.

Cornetist Rex Stewart showed the influence of both Armstrong and Beiderbecke in his work with Fletcher Henderson and (later) Duke Ellington.

The birth of jazz vocals

Other trumpet players and other instrumentalists were not the only ones to be inspired by Louis Armstrong, for Armstrong had always considered himself a singer as well as a trumpeter. Popular singing was never the same after Armstrong opened an interpretive door through which jazz and pop vocalists – as well as country and rock singers – would pass.

In addition to being the most influential instrumental soloist in jazz, Louis Armstrong the vocalist shaped all of the popular music that followed.

The Hot Five and Hot Seven recordings revealed a rough, spontaneous approach to singing and a knack for melodic and rhythmic embellishment that matched the creativity of Armstrong's trumpet choruses. A popular Hot Five recording, 'Heebie Jeebies' from 1926, features a wordless vocal chorus, scat singing. Armstrong didn't invent scat, despite his claim to have generated the technique on-the-spot after dropping the lyric sheet in the recording studio, but his popularization of the approach clarified the songlike nature of improvisation and suggested the creative potential jazz held for singers as well as players.

After moving to New York again in 1929, Armstrong was able to realize this potential on the more widely accessible terrain of the popular song. Black artists were rarely allowed to record popular fare when Armstrong cut 'I Can't Give You Anything But Love' in March 1929. The impact of both his playing and his singing on this title was so great that within months his records, now invariably including vocal as well as trumpet choruses, were turning the best new songs of the day into standards.

The vocal influence

While critical analysis tends to place far more emphasis on Armstrong's trumpet, the effect of his singing proved equally profound. In a flash, he destroyed notions of stiff-backed vocal propriety, introducing nuances and inflections that could transform a trite set of lyrics into caustic social commentary or existential epic. While several of his earliest vocal recordings are among his most profound (including 'Ain't Misbehavin'', 'Stardust' and 'Lazy River'), several efforts from later periods, including 'Thanks a Million' and 'Once in a While', despite more pedestrian orchestrations, are also tremendously moving.

The impact of Armstrong the vocalist was felt far and wide. Trumpeters who shared his New Orleans' background (Henry 'Red' Allen, Joseph 'Wingy' Manone and Louis Prima) quickly became singing trumpeters in his wake, compounding Armstrong's image as the new music's emblematic figure. Singers of varied backgrounds were also falling under Armstrong's influence. Bing Crosby, for one, had begun to emulate Armstrong's scatting in 1927, when he recorded as one of Paul Whiteman's Rhythm Boys. He quickly adapted the speechlike aspects of Armstrong's pop recordings to create the crooning style that turned Crosby into the most successful singer of the 1930s. Mildred Bailey, like Crosby a native of Washington State (and the sister of another Rhythm Boy), stayed closer to jazz and became the music's first important female vocalist after joining forces with her husband Red Norvo.

must know

Louis Armstrong introduced scat singing to the public on a popular 1926 recording by the Hot Five.

Mildred Bailey, the first great female jazz vocalist.

Vocalists and small groups

Popular singers Bing Crosby and Mildred Bailey worked primarily in front of orchestras, while the two most important black singers to follow Armstrong's path in the 1930s – the legendary Fats Waller and Billie Holiday – did their best work with smaller groups.

did you know?

Thanks to years of playing accompaniments to silent films, Fats Waller mastered the pipe organ and recorded the first jazz solos on the instrument.

Fats Waller

Singing was only one of Thomas 'Fats' Waller's talents. He was an extraordinary pianist, the master of the stride style pioneered by older players such as James P. Johnson and Willie 'The Lion' Smith. This style featured a left hand moving between emphatic bass notes and rich chords. He was also a successful composer, turning out classic instrumental originals and, in collaboration with lyricist Andy Razaf, hit songs including 'Ain't Misbehavin'' and 'Honeysuckle Rose'.

From 1934 until his death in 1943, he was best known for the extensive series of sextet recordings by Fats Waller and His Rhythm that mocked the pretensions of the period's popular music. Waller's broad readings of often inconsequential material,

Thomas 'Fats' Waller, exuding good times alone at the piano (*below*) and at the helm of his popular small ensemble (*below right*).

and the mugging that was captured in several short films, may appear to be racist relics upon first encounter, but Waller himself was never the butt of the jokes, and his acerbic interpretations elevated his material while always managing to swing like crazy.

Billie Holiday

Billie Holiday swung as well, but she found a bittersweet and often frustrated passion in her material. Where Waller made you laugh, Holiday broke your heart, creating subtexts with an improvisational delivery that made each chorus unpredictable and deeply moving. Seeming to wear her own troubled history on her sleeve, and conveying an aura of both vulnerability and determination, she quickly gained attention through the small-group recordings that pianist Teddy Wilson began leading in 1935. A year later, Holiday launched a concurrent series under her own name that proved equally definitive. When she decided to record a poem about a southern lynching called 'Strange Fruit' in 1939, however, her record company rejected the notion, and she was forced to take what became one of her signature songs to the newly formed independent Commodore label.

Armstrong's statement about the American racial climate a decade earlier was the Waller/Razaf 'Black and Blue'. This ballad was originally designed as a dark-skinned woman's lament after being frustrated by a 'high yellow' rival, but Armstrong transformed it into an anthem of racial dignity. His artistry was such that Armstrong could take the sting out of the racist lyrics to 'Shine' and 'Shoe Shine Boy', his range great enough to spawn 1930 collaboration with country music pioneer Jimmie Rogers on 'Blue Yodel No. 9'.

Billie Holiday, known as 'Lady Day', one of the music's most influential and iconic figures.

Armstrong in the 1930s

As the 1930s progressed, Louis Armstrong became a familiar presence on radio and in films, a true American celebrity and an international star. Composition and arrangement were the only areas where Armstrong didn't dominate jazz – those were more the realm of Jelly Roll Morton and his Red Hot Peppers.

did you know?

In 1930s' Europe, black musicians enjoyed more work and – if not true equality – a more polite form of discrimination.

Armstrong spent 18 months in Europe during 1933 and 1934 to escape a management dispute involving New York and Chicago factions with underworld connections. His business problems were ultimately resolved when Joe Glaser became his permanent manager in 1935, but other musicians had taken note of Armstrong's reception on the Continent. With both Depression economics and old-fashioned racism limiting prospects at home, leading musicians including Coleman Hawkins and Benny Carter were soon making their own temporary escape to Europe. When they arrived they found a small but growing number of European musicians who were struggling to master the jazz language.

Django Reinhardt

The greatest of these was Django Reinhardt, the gypsy guitarist who overcame childhood injuries to his left hand and created the first influential jazz style outside of America. The recordings of the Quintette of the Hot Club of France, which featured Reinhardt and violinist Stephane Grappelli, brought the guitarist immediate international acclaim, which grew after he encountered Hawkins, Carter and other American expatriates on a series of recordings.

Armstrong in his prime, playing his first instrument, the cornet.

Jazz as a written art

While Armstrong invented brilliant melodies on the spot and copyrighted a handful of songs under his own name, he was not inclined to labour over written music and did not orchestrate. A flair for structure and organization that Armstrong lacked was required to make jazz a composer's as well as a player's medium. These were the very traits that made Jelly Roll Morton's Red Hot Peppers recordings of 1926–28 so significant.

The Red Hot Peppers

Morton had already recorded as a piano soloist and as a guest of the New Orleans Rhythm Kings, but the Red Hot Peppers recordings he made for the Victor label in Chicago and New York gave the first and best indications of his ensemble concepts. While the small groups assembled on these occasions looked like King Oliver's Creole Jazz Band and other New Orleans ensembles, and each player had an opportunity within the arrangements to improvise variations on the written material, the musical results were closer to orchestrated versions of Morton's piano solos.

Each performance was a study in dramatic contrast that Morton specifically conceived and dictated to the musicians in every particular. Morton varied his written melodies with breaks, pithy solos, collective improvisations and shifts in the underlying rhythms. His use of multiple themes in a single piece harkened back to the ragtime composers, even as the liberties he took with these themes and his sleeker and more mobile beat took his music beyond ragtime's formalities. The several talented musicians in the Red Hot Peppers were present to

Django Reinhardt was the first great non-American jazz musician.

The Red Hot Peppers perform, with leader Jelly Roll Morton at the piano.

realize Morton's concepts rather than to stand out on their own. Unlike an Armstrong Hot Five or Hot Seven, the whole of a Red Hot Peppers performance such as 'Black Bottom Stomp' or 'Dead Man Blues' really was greater than the sum of its parts.

Unfortunately for Morton, musical tastes had moved on by the time he was able to document his small band ideas on record. The more open-ended collective playing on simpler blues themes by Oliver's Creole Jazz Band had already popularized a later New Orleans approach, while the virtuosity of an improvising soloist like Armstrong was another matter entirely. These changes didn't deter the obstreperous Morton from insisting that his way was the only true way, but they did ensure that he would slip further into obscurity as Armstrong's influence took hold and big bands came to dominate the music.

Jelly's last jams

Morton was managing a club in Washington, D.C., when Alan Lomax found him in 1938 and recorded a lengthy series of the pianist's reminiscences, complete with musical illustrations, for the Library of Congress. Though characteristically slanted to aggrandize his contributions, these monologues were the first significant example of jazz oral history. The interviews also created sufficient interest to allow Lomax to record a valedictory series of band sessions with old friends Red Allen, Sidney Bechet, Albert Nicholas and Arthur 'Zutty' Singleton featured, plus sagacious solo performances that capture Morton the pianist and vocalist a year prior to his 1941 passing.

Morton near the end, still cantankerous and still claiming the role of jazz's prime mover.

Duke Ellington

Jazz's greatest composer and arranger was Edward Kennedy 'Duke' Ellington. From his initial development as a pianist to the creation of his orchestra, Ellington displayed a style so individual that it has rarely been seriously imitated. His radio broadcasts from Harlem's Cotton Club in the late 1920s helped to spread his music across America and made him a jazz figure second in popularity only to Louis Armstrong.

Born in 1899, Duke Ellington enjoyed as close to a middle-class upbringing as an African American could experience in segregated Washington. Raised in an atmosphere of culture, he originally planned to become a commercial artist, but he grew fascinated with the piano music of James P. Johnson, which he taught himself from piano rolls Johnson had produced.

By the time Ellington finished high school, he was developing a reputation as a pianist, composing his own feature tunes and leading small combos. Ellington relocated to New York in 1923, and over the next four years he built a band that would grow to ten

Duke Ellington, or 'the piano player' as he often dismissively referred to himself.

pieces during an extended engagement at a speakeasy alternately known as the Hollywood Café and the Kentucky Club. Ellington taught himself harmony and orchestration through trial and error. He moved beyond his initial enthusiasm for stride piano and the grand flourishes of popular white dance orchestras to the challenges of jazz as played by southern black musicians.

By Ellington's own account, the catalyst was Sidney Bechet, with whom he collaborated briefly in 1925. Already attuned to notions of racial pride and black culture as a result of his upbringing in Washington, Ellington was fascinated by Bechet's use of the blues and improvisation, much as Ernst Ansermet had been six years earlier.

Building the Ellington Orchestra

Bechet was not available to become a permanent member of his orchestra, but Ellington began to expand his ensemble of old Washington friends and schoolmates by adding such key players from the South as bassist Wellman Braud and clarinetist Barney Bigard (both New Orleans natives) and South Carolina trumpeter James 'Bubber' Miley. The point was not to present an urbanized version of southern music, but rather to capture American Negro life in all of its variations. Boston saxophonists

Duke Ellington and his orchestra *circa* **1940, after time and success had allowed it to reach twice its original size.**

Harry Carney and Johnny Hodges and New York trombonist Joe 'Tricky Sam' Nanton, other late 1920s' arrivals, became equally essential components of the Ellington mix.

The orchestra as instrument

Ellington could take exercise figures and throwaway phrases that the members of his band played and turn them into such classic songs as 'Mood Indigo', based on a pattern Bigard employed while warming up. Entire arrangements were built around such maverick sounds as the growls that Miley and Nanton obtained when using bathroom plungers to mute their horns. Some have claimed that Ellington took credit for ideas and entire compositions that originated with his sidemen, yet the cliché that the orchestra was Ellington's true instrument is closer to the mark. Musicians sounded different (and generally better) when playing under Ellington's leadership for the same reason that other arrangers found it so difficult to re-create the Ellington style – because Ellington was writing not simply notes to be played by interchangeable musicians, but sounds that were a direct reflection of a specific combination of individuals.

The public became aware of Ellington once he moved uptown to the Cotton Club late in 1927. This Harlem nightspot, which catered to slumming downtown whites and did not admit black customers, had floorshows with an African theme. Ellington's

The very pose of bandleader Cab Calloway suggests the theatricality that was a key component of the music created for the Cotton Club.

use of such exotic touches as raucous brass figures, mysterious low reed voicings and (on 'Creole Love Call') even the wordless singing of a female vocalist only furthered the effect. His style became known as 'jungle music', and the band even released some records under the name The Jungle Band.

Cotton Club and radio

Early Ellington classics cut before the band moved to the Cotton Club, especially 'East St Louis Toodle-oo' and 'Black and Tan Fantasy', had already set the tone and begun to build the orchestra's reputation. The Cotton Club provided the added feature of regular live broadcasts over that new home-entertainment phenomenon, the radio. Until his tenure at the club ended in 1931, Ellington's 'remote' broadcasts helped to spread his music across America and made him a jazz figure second in popularity only to Armstrong.

Ellington matures

Never content merely to dispense ersatz primitivism, Ellington developed a world in sound over the next decade. Riff-based pieces like 'Rockin' in Rhythm' (1930) and 'It Don't Mean a Thing (If It Ain't Got That Swing)' (1932) anticipated the coming swing craze. 'Mood Indigo' (1930), 'Sophisticated Lady' (1933) and 'Solitude' (1934) were haunting ballads that gained even greater popularity after lyrics were added. Two 1936 works, 'Echoes of Harlem' (for Miley's successor, trumpeter Charles 'Cootie' Williams) and 'Clarinet Lament' (for Bigard), introduced the concept of mini-concertos for individual soloists. Each new composition created a

Cootie Williams inherited the important featured trumpet chair in Ellington's orchestra from Bubber Miley.

vivid image of life as Ellington and his musicians knew it, and none of his early music was more vivid than his first attempts at extended composition, 'Creole Rhapsody' (1931) and 'Reminiscing in Tempo' (1935).

The Duke at 40

For a time after big band swing became popular in the late 1930s, Ellington's more ambitious music seemed to diverge from popular taste, yet he persevered, producing brilliant and diverse new works at a superhuman pace. By 1940 three important new contributors had joined his orchestra – Ben Webster, the first star tenor saxophone soloist to be featured in the band; Jimmie Blanton, the revolutionary young bassist; and Billy Strayhorn, a songwriter from Pittsburgh, who would become Ellington's most valuable collaborator over the next 30 years – and Ellington was in the midst of his most creative period.

Don Redman and Chick Webb

Ellington's approach, built upon the often-eccentric sound of his musicians plus his own magical ability to blend these sounds in new ways, was too personal and complex to become the norm for jazz orchestras. The strategies Don Redman introduced with Fletcher Henderson – setting section against section, often in call-and-response exchanges; varying thematic phrases known as riffs to underscore and offset improvised solos – were easier to grasp and as a result became widely imitated.

Redman refined the style with McKinney's Cotton Pickers, the band he joined as musical director after leaving Henderson in 1927, and in later groups under his own name. William 'Chick' Webb, a

must know

'Everything had a picture or was descriptive of something', Duke Ellington once explained.

Chick Webb, one of the first great jazz drummers and big band leaders.

small, hunchbacked drummer from Baltimore, added such a propulsive beat to the orchestra he led that, from 1927 until his death twelve years later, it consistently prevailed over all competitors in band 'battles' held at Webb's Harlem base, the Savoy Ballroom. From 1933 on, Webb benefited from the contributions of arranger/composer Edgar Sampson, who wrote the classic 'Stompin' at the Savoy'.

Two-beat and 4/4 time

While Webb's band made its name playing for dancers at the ballroom known as 'The Home of Happy Feet', the band of Jimmie Lunceford garnered more attention for the tightly choreographed flourishes of its stage shows, in which the trumpeters would toss and then catch their horns in unison and several members would temporarily abandon their instruments for 'glee club' vocals and dance routines. The ensemble performed with similar precision when playing the arrangements of pianist Ed Wilcox and trumpeter Melvin 'Sy' Oliver, employing a crisp two-beat rhythmic feeling that became a Lunceford trademark. Both the swing and the ensemble execution were looser in the great Kansas City bands of Bennie Moten and Andy Kirk and the Walter Page Blue Devils of Oklahoma City, which by 1930 were introducing a more flowing feeling into the music.

Ensemble precision and showmanship helped make Jimmie Lunceford's orchestra one of jazz's premier ensembles in the 1930s.

Big bands in the mainstream

The freedom that jazz offered to large ensembles led musicians with common backgrounds to adopt a variety of musical strategies. As a rule, it was the white musicians who were learning lessons from their black counterparts, and no white musician of the period absorbed the jazz spirit more thoroughly, or to greater public impact, than clarinetist Benny Goodman.

Swing Era precursors

Paul Whiteman continued to present a hodgepodge of music, hiring talented jazz players including trumpeter Rowland 'Bunny' Berigan and trombonist Jack Teagarden and then giving them limited feature space. Other white bands were taking jazz more seriously. The Casa Loma Orchestra became widely popular with college audiences for boldly rhythmic pieces including 'Casa Loma Stomp' and 'San Sue Strut' that reflected the influence of Henderson and Redman. Gene Gifford, the band's primary arranger, wrote pieces called 'White Jazz', 'Black Jazz' and 'Blues Jazz' to show the music was becoming a multihued enterprise.

The Casa Loma Orchestra brought jazz to a young white audience, anticipating the swing music craze to come.

Benny Goodman and clarinet – the
man and the instrument
that launched the Swing Era.

Benny Goodman

Benny Goodman spent the first portion of his career perfecting his instrumental command and his demanding musicianship in his hometown Chicago (where he heard many of the New Orleans masters as well as Beiderbecke), in a tour with drummer Ben Pollack's Orchestra that reached California, and finally during a half-dozen productive years as a freelance musician in the radio and recording studios of New York. By 1934 Goodman was ready to organize his own big band; by the end of 1935, the Goodman band was a pop music phenomenon, and the Swing Era was born.

The importance of black arrangers

Many leading soloists played in Goodman's band during the remainder of the decade, including a few (trumpeters Berigan and Harry James, drummer Gene Krupa) who were able to launch successful bands of their own. Yet the key to Goodman's success was the writing, contributed by such leading arrangers as Benny Carter, Fletcher Henderson and Edgar Sampson. Many of their most popular works had already been recorded by Henderson ('King Porter Stomp', 'Down South Camp Meetin'') or Chick Webb ('Stompin' at the Savoy', 'Don't Be That Way'), albeit without the crispness and pinpoint execution that Goodman demanded.

Radio ignites the swing phenomenon

Beginning in November 1934, Goodman's band had been featured on the NBC network programme *Let's Dance*, which aired at at 9 p.m. in California and at midnight in East Coast cities. This time difference

must know

Benny Goodman's
big band was the
most jazz-attuned of
his white studio
counterparts, often
playing scores by
leading black arrangers.

explains the unexpected riot that greeted Goodman when he opened with one of Henderson's arrangements at Los Angeles's Palomar Ballroom in August 1935. His prime-time West Coast broadcasts had been heard by young dancers before their East Coast counterparts discovered what came to be known as swing music. Word spread quickly once Goodman began recording prolifically for RCA Victor, moved to the earlier *Camel Caravan* programme on the CBS network, and made film appearances in *The Big Broadcast of 1937* and other features. Soon teenagers were also rioting at the Paramount Theater in New York, while the aloof and temperamental Goodman was hailed as the King of Swing.

King or thief?

Goodman and other studio veterans who went on to Swing Era success, including Tommy and Jimmy Dorsey, Artie Shaw and Glenn Miller, were excellent musicians. Goodman was also an excellent improviser, with an honest rhythmic flair and a personal feeling for the popular songs of the period. The interest he generated in big bands also led to a wider hearing for black bandleaders, including Webb, Lunceford and the flamboyant Cab Calloway. Yet the cultural double standard that placed Goodman at the pinnacle of an African American musical style has led many observers and musicians to conclude that his success was not honestly gained, that he had 'stolen' jazz (as Elvis Presley would later be accused of stealing rhythm and blues). It is closer to the truth to credit Goodman for appreciating jazz more than most of his Caucasian contemporaries, and applying his own personality to the music more successfully.

must know

Goodman combined a discipline in ensemble and abandon in solos that the general public embraced. He brought jazz as close as it would ever come to a position of dominance in popular music.

must know

Benny Goodman would have never realized his triumph without the assistance of radio.

The urge to integrate

Jazz hadn't been a racially exclusive enterprise since its youth in New Orleans, and jazz musicians had begun ignoring colour lines long before the rest of American society. But the Benny Goodman Quartet brought integration front and centre while opening up opportunities for musicians to showcase their talents in a small-group format.

did you know?

'Knockin' a Jug' was the first recorded meeting between trumpeter Louis Armstrong and trombone giant Jack Teagarden.

The years prior to Benny Goodman's initial success were dotted with examples of interracial collaboration in the recording studio, including the New Orleans Rhythm Kings/Jelly Roll Morton encounter of 1923 and Louis Armstrong's 1929 'Knockin' a Jug'. In the Mound City Blues Blowers recordings of the same year, Coleman Hawkins stood shoulder to shoulder with Glenn Miller and Charles 'Pee Wee' Russell. And a stunning 1932 series by a group called the Rhythmakers found New Orleans giants Red Allen and Zutty Singleton joining forces with Russell, Gene Krupa and Tommy Dorsey. In featuring the music of black arrangers in his live performances, Goodman simply made this connection more overt.

Integration on the bandstand

Goodman did far more when he and Krupa began recording and then performing live with pianist Teddy Wilson and vibraphonist Lionel Hampton in the Benny Goodman Trio and Quartet. Black and white musicians on stage together was a radical statement in 1936, integration with a vengeance. Hampton stated in 1994 that 'the Benny Goodman

The musically and socially seminal Benny Goodman Quartet, with vibist Lionel Hampton, pianist Teddy Wilson and drummer Gene Krupa.

Quartet opened the door for Jackie Robinson coming into major league baseball. The integration of musicians started a lot of things happening'.

Small groups in the big band era

The Quartet's success also created a bit of space, at least in the recording studios, for smaller jazz units. A few of these combos managed to sustain a performing career during the peak of big bands, including Fats Waller's Rhythm, the similarly ebullient Onyx Club Boys that violinist Hezekiah 'Stuff' Smith led on Manhattan's 52nd Street, and the more refined sextet of bassist John Kirby, which interpreted

must know

The racially integrated Goodman combo, which played feature segments during the big band's performances, has been cited as one of the first salvos of the civil rights movement.

John Kirby's sextet was called 'the biggest little band in the land'.

Pianist Teddy Wilson became highly influential through his work in Benny Goodman's small groups and the recording sessions under his own name that made Billie Holiday a star.

classical material as well as more typical riff tunes. Yet big band sounds continued to dominate, and instrumental soloists who worked in the big bands rarely found opportunities to display their full talents within the confines of arrangements generally designed to feature vocalists and to highlight the power of the full ensemble.

As a result, many musicians are best remembered today for their work in small bands assembled specifically for recordings. Teddy Wilson, the Goodman Trio/Quartet pianist, led one such series on the Brunswick label that initially established Billie Holiday. Goodman Quartet vibist Lionel Hampton created an equally imposing small-group discography on RCA Victor's Bluebird subsidiary. Both leaders were able to draw upon musicians from the best black and white swing bands, and what resulted (as with the Hot Five and Hot Seven a decade earlier) is a picture of the era quite different from the nightly working norm. Leon 'Chu' Berry, for one example, was a star tenor saxophone soloist with Cab Calloway's orchestra yet may be better known historically for the recordings he cut with Wilson and Hampton.

The true king of swing

A new infusion of talent, not to mention the true epitome of swing, was injected into the national scene when William 'Count' Basie brought his orchestra east from Kansas City at the end of 1936. One of the orchestra's stars was hip saxophonist Lester Young who, along with other jazz visionaries of the late 1930s, anticipated the modern sounds that would shortly follow.

Basie had been the featured pianist with bassist Walter Page's Blue Devils, a group second to none in its interpretations of blues material and one of the first to streamline jazz rhythm into a smoother 4/4 feeling. Basie, Page and Page's star singer Jimmy Rushing ultimately joined Bennie Moten, Kansas City's top bandleader. When Moten died in 1935, Basie took these key players and added others, including tenor saxophonist Lester Young and drummer Jo Jones, to create his own group.

The Basie band was looser in its beat and its approach to orchestration, since it relied less upon written arrangements than improvised riffs created

did you know?

Count Basie, a native of New Jersey, had been stranded in the Midwest by a failed vaudeville tour in 1927.

Count Basie acknowledges the crowd.

by the sections on the bandstand and then memorized (hence the term 'head arrangement', meaning something remembered rather than committed to paper). Producer John Hammond, who among other things would become Goodman's brother-in-law, grew so excited upon hearing a Basie radio broadcast in Chicago that he drove straight to Kansas City and persuaded Basie to head east. While the public initially considered Basie's approach too rough-and-tumble, his lean reduction of the current style typified what 'territory' bands in the Midwest and Southwest had been doing for several years, and established musicians including Goodman (who had a bigger hit with Basie's theme 'One O'clock Jump' than Basie himself) were quick to catch on.

Lester Young

The Basie band would have been important if all it had done was to introduce the world to the magical Lester Young. The tenor saxophone was Young's primary instrument, although he did not play it in the brawny, aggressive style that Coleman Hawkins had created. Young's lighter tone, which bore the mark of white saxophonists Jimmy Dorsey and Frankie Trumbauer, and his oblique manner of phrasing seemed other-worldly in comparison and had led him to a disastrous experience in 1934 when he briefly replaced Hawkins in Fletcher Henderson's band.

Musical and cultural influence

Kansas City and the new Basie group were more welcoming, and by 1936, when Young made his first recordings in a small group called Jones-Smith, Inc., the jazz world was better prepared to absorb his

must know

Lester Young was one of the most original voices in jazz history and, despite his legendary status, still one of the most underrated.

discoveries. Through featured recordings with Basie, several immortal sessions in support of Billie Holiday, and the Kansas City Five and Six titles that featured his clarinet, Young became the most unique and influential solo voice since Armstrong. An eccentric individual who coined his own vernacular and carried himself with an air of aloof diffidence, Young was also the prototypical hipster, and his personal affectations had a profound influence on the subsequent Beat Generation. It was Young's music, however, that made the greatest impact, anticipating the modern sounds that would shortly follow.

Harbingers of things to come

Other visionaries were at work as the 1930s ended. Pianist Art Tatum, as elaborate in his conception as Young was terse, presented another array of possibilities. Tatum's solo recordings revealed a technique exceeding that of most great concert pianists, a highly refined keyboard touch and a sophisticated sense of harmony. They both summarized the approach of Tatum's idol Fats Waller and revealed a new realm for the improvising musician. While no one could duplicate Tatum's keyboard virtuosity, his rich harmonies and ability to improvise at supersonic tempos suggested much of what jazz would achieve in the near future. Other new sounds in the air included the polyrhythm of drummer Kenny Clarke, the angular leaps of trumpeter John 'Dizzy' Gillespie, the penetrating sound and riff-based ease of electric guitar pioneer Charlie Christian (who joined Goodman in 1939), and the unprecedented mobility and tonal strength of bassist Jimmie Blanton (who was added to the Ellington Orchestra in the same year).

Musicians would declare that 'God is in the house' when pianist Art Tatum arrived at a jam session.

Charlie Christian died young but lived long enough to popularize the sound of the electric guitar.

Jazz gets serious

Such innovations were timely, since jazz was turning the corner from its status as novel popular fad to serious art form. Carnegie Hall bookings and the emergence of several independent record labels with a jazz focus were signs that the music was beginning to be taken more seriously. By the end of the decade, younger artists were ready to take the music to new places.

Among Goodman's achievements was the presentation of jazz in the concert hall.

Paul Whiteman had tried to effect jazz's transition from fad to art form, to 'make a lady of jazz' as the cliché has it, in a 1924 concert at New York's Aeolian Hall. That event included both the ODJB playing 'Wang Wang Blues' with the Whiteman orchestra and the premiere of George Gershwin's jazz-influenced 'Rhapsody in Blue'. Yet it was Benny Goodman who made the point more effectively in 1938, when his first Carnegie Hall concert was built around a mini-history of jazz, with assists from members of the Ellington and Basie bands. A second sequence of influential Carnegie Hall concerts, Spirituals to Swing, began in the following year and took an even more inclusive view by placing gospel choirs, country blues singers and boogie-woogie pianists on the same bill with Goodman and Basie.

Independent record labels

A few pioneering entrepreneurs were intent on documenting the small-band music that had been eclipsed by the popularity of swing orchestras. Many of these producers considered big bands less than authentic in the jazz realm and dedicated themselves to recording the music in its purer setting; most could not afford to pay large ensembles in any event.

Milt Gabler's Commodore label, launched on the morning after Goodman's Carnegie Hall debut, began with an emphasis on such white Chicago musicians as Eddie Condon and Pee Wee Russell, who had never been comfortable in big bands, then expanded its reach by also taping Young, Hawkins, trumpet star Roy Eldridge and other important black musicians. Alfred Lion's Blue Note got its start in the wake of a Spirituals to Swing concert with extended performances by boogie-woogie pianists Albert Ammons and Meade Lux Lewis, then moved on to small-band recordings by the still elusive Sidney Bechet.

Other imprints, like the Hot Record Society (HRS), were created to reissue obscure titles from the previous decade. The larger Columbia label followed suit in 1940, when Yale College student George Avakian persuaded executives to return Armstrong's Hot Five and Hot Seven classics to its catalogue. At the same time, trumpeter Muggsy Spanier demonstrated the ongoing viability of the early jazz repertoire in 1939 Bluebird recordings by his Ragtimers, and authors Fred Ramsey and Bill Russell introduced the world to the man they claimed to be Armstrong's progenitor, the then-inactive Willie 'Bunk' Johnson, in their book of the same year, *Jazzmen*.

The next wave

The preference of many popular bands, especially those of Tommy Dorsey and Glenn Miller, for more commercial arrangements that emphasized 'sweet' vocal choruses would lead to a de-emphasis on rhythmic power in popular music. A harbinger of this

Early independent labels, and those that followed in the 1940s such as Musicraft, heralded things to come in both musical and business realms.

change, though one who in time would prove capable of swinging quite effectively, was the young Frank Sinatra, still relatively unknown when he moved from the band of Harry James to Dorsey's more successful group in 1940.

Changes of a far different order were promised when Charlie Parker, another product of the heady Kansas City milieu, discovered a provocative new way to approach rhythm and harmony while jamming in the kitchen of a Harlem restaurant in 1939. These sounds announced that swing, which Armstrong had made the *lingua franca* of American music, had not been depleted by the Swing Era, although the directions that jazz was poised to pursue would not always remain identified with the term.

Charlie Parker was poised to take jazz beyond the Swing Era as the 1930s ended.

want to know more?

The songs listed below, along with the musicians or groups who performed them, are some of the highlights of the era.

- Louis Armstrong
  'Ain't Misbehavin''
  'Cornet Chop Suey'
  'Heebie Jeebies'
  'Lazy River'
  'Potato Head Blues'
  'Stardust'
  'Struttin' with Some Barbecue'
  'Weather Bird'
  'West End Blues'
- Mildred Bailey
  'Rockin' Chair'
- Count Basie
  'Blue and Sentimental'
  'One O'Clock Jump'
  'Sent for You Yesterday'
  'Swingin' the Blues'
- Bix Beiderbecke
  'In a Mist'
  'Singing the Blues'
- Chu Berry
  'Sittin' In'
- Casa Loma Orchestra
  'San Sue Strut'
- Charlie Christian with Benny Goodman
  'Breakfast Feud'
- Duke Ellington's Orchestra
  'Black and Tan Fantasy'
  'Caravan'
  'It Don't Mean a Thing '
  'Mood Indigo'
  'Reminiscing in Tempo'
  'Solitude'
- Benny Goodman
  'Body and Soul'
  'King Porter Stomp'
  'Sing, Sing, Sing'
- Coleman Hawkins
  'Body and Soul'
- Fletcher Henderson's Orchestra
  'Down South Camp Meetin''
  'King Porter Stomp'
  'Somebody Loves Me'
  'Sugarfoot Stomp'
- Billie Holiday
  'All of Me'
  'Foolin' Myself'
  'Strange Fruit'
- Jones-Smith, Inc. (Lester Young)
  'Lady Be Good'
- John Kirby
  'Undecided'
- Jimmie Lunceford
  'For Dancers Only'
  'Organ Grinder Swing'
- McKenzie & Condon's Chicagoans
  'Nobody's Sweetheart'
- Jelly Roll Morton's Red Hot Peppers
  'Black Bottom Stomp'
  'Dead Man Blues'
- King Oliver's Creole Jazz Band
  'Chimes Blues'
  'Dipper Mouth Blues'
- Quintette du Hot Club (Django Reinhardt)
  'Avalon'
- Bessie Smith
  'Back Water Blues'
  'St Louis Blues'
- Mamie Smith
  'Crazy Blues'
- Art Tatum
  'Tea for Two'
  'Tiger Rag'
- Fats Waller
  'Ain't Misbehavin''
  'Honeysuckle Rose'
- William 'Chick' Webb
  'Stompin' at the Savoy'
- Paul Whiteman
  'Rhapsody in Blue'

3 Bebop hard and cool (1941–1960)

The decline of the big band, and of jazz's status as popular music, was precipitous. When the 1940s began, the creativity and commercial success of Benny Goodman, Artie Shaw, Duke Ellington and Count Basie appeared beyond challenge; yet when World War II ended in 1945, the big band era was clearly waning and 'swing music' appeared passé. Ways of life were changing, and the music was changing as well, along a variety of paths that made questions of what was and was not jazz knottier than ever.

What killed the big bands?

People began to speak of the orchestras that remained as dinosaurs. By 1946, when Goodman, Tommy Dorsey, Harry James, Les Brown and Woody Herman (the last at the peak of his innovative influence) all gave up on the road and on the maintenance of permanent ensembles, it was clear that an era had passed.

Glenn Miller, the most popular big band leader of the early 1940s, in his final 'band' uniform.

Even without considering the development of new musical styles, we can identify several factors that worked against sustaining the public's passion for swing. The war took numerous significant musicians out of circulation, including Glenn Miller, who sustained his popularity by leading an Armed Forces band in Europe until a plane in which he travelled was lost while crossing the English Channel in 1944. Those bands still touring in the United States had to face petrol rationing, a shortage of vinyl, the imposition of a new cabaret tax that impacted live performances, and what amounted to a quarantine on new 78s.

Meanwhile, in the summer of 1942 the American Federation of Musicians, in an effort to secure royalties, declared a ban on the recording of instrumentalists. Singers, who were not members of the AFM, continued to turn out new records, often accompanied by vocal choruses rather than orchestras, while players went undocumented from the beginning of the ban until their respective record labels made peace with the union one-by-one a year or two later.

People were settling into a new, often suburban lifestyle that, with the advent of television, would soon create serious adjustments in America's social habits. 'After the war', bandleader Les Brown explained, 'guys came back and settled down with their families, and the ballrooms went to hell. Before the war, every town with 20,000 people had a ballroom. We could spend a month doing one-nighters just in Texas'. If the music had done nothing but remain fixed along the lines of its pre-war conventions, these surrounding factors would have made change inevitable.

New trends in music

Where big band jazz had achieved its commercial prominence as dance music, the new sounds of small combos and the bold creations of the remaining orchestras often strayed far from a dance beat. At the same time, trends in the popular music that supplanted big bands diverged from the flowing 4/4 jazz tempo.

Such developments present a challenge for those who wish to portray succeeding styles of American music as branches emanating from a common jazz tree. The roots truly sprawled in the 1940s, bringing forth new hybrids that only occasionally twined back to the main jazz branch.

Smaller ensembles would lead the way in the 1940s, including this combo led by pianist Tadd Dameron and featuring trumpeter Fats Navarro.

Dizzy Gillespie continued to place his trumpet in front of a big band, which introduced such stars as pianist John Lewis, saxophonist James Moody (with glasses) and bassist Ray Brown.

What killed the big bands? | 75

Vocalists to the forefront

Vocalists were always critical to the success of the big bands, even when the bands were also known for the brilliance of their arrangements and soloists. In the 1940s such stars as Frank Sinatra, Nat Cole and Ella Fitzgerald eclipsed their supporting bands and became the focus of popular attention.

must know

The reigning pop vocalists – Bing Crosby in the 1930s and Frank Sinatra in the 1940s – were heavily influenced by jazz. But their greatest successes had little to do with the jazz side of their personalities.

The success of Frank Sinatra led to the overshadowing of big bands by big band vocalists.

Thanks to the popularity of the swing beat and the influence of Louis Armstrong, many band vocalists displayed obvious jazz feeling. Yet even at the height of the swing era, large segments of the public craved a more saccharine and sentimental approach to vocals that might be considered pre-Armstrong. Orchestras were often categorized as either swing bands or sweet bands to underscore the distinction.

Frank Sinatra and jazz-influenced pop

Frank Sinatra was featured with Dorsey's band between 1940 and 1942 and was heavily influenced by the trombonist's phrasing, as well as by the rhythmic attack and emotional nuances of Armstrong and Billie Holiday. The pandemonium that greeted the launch of Sinatra's solo career at the close of 1942, when his in-person accompaniment emphasized string orchestrations rather than the big band sound, was among the clearest signs that swing was already in commercial jeopardy.

Sinatra was clearly the definitive pop vocalist of the 1940s and 1950s. He was able to reverse a temporary decline in popularity with an Oscar-winning performance in the film *From Here to*

Eternity and a subsequent series of albums for Capitol Records. While he worked with jazz musicians such as trumpeter Harry 'Sweets' Edison on his recordings, and while 'swinging' became a trademark mood (as on his classic album *Songs for Swinging Lovers*), Sinatra rarely improvised or stressed the rhythmic side of his talents.

Jazz vocalists transition to pop

Nat Cole began his career as a highly influential trio pianist whose style linked the linear explorations of Earl Hines with a more streamlined flow. He gained additional popularity with riff-based vocals before attaining superstar status by virtually abandoning piano playing to concentrate on a relaxed ballad style surrounded by lush orchestrations. Billy Eckstine, who sang the blues with Hines and then played trumpet and valve trombone in a band of his own that featured such innovators as Charlie Parker and Dizzy Gillespie, began to favour ballads and more conservative arrangements once he was hailed as 'the Sepia Sinatra'.

Ella Fitzgerald initially found fame singing novelty songs with Chick Webb, then embraced more sophisticated jazz ideas with her virtuoso approach to scat singing. But she enjoyed her greatest popular success with lushly arranged 'songbook' albums on the Verve label dedicated to the great pop composers, albums that (together with Sinatra's Capitol recordings) defined those songs considered 'standards'. Thus was the nature of non-rock popular music set by the 1950s, and even singers with unimpeachable jazz credentials such as Sarah Vaughan and Dinah Washington were frequently led into its calmer waters.

Nat 'King' Cole was a popular and influential pianist and trio leader before becoming a vocal superstar.

Billy Eckstine played occasional trombone and led an important big band but is best remembered for his success singing love songs.

Rhythm and blues, rock and roll

These same singers, and Sinatra as well, also would occasionally succumb to the pull of rock and roll as the 1950s progressed. This side of popular music displayed clearer roots in the blues, especially in the vocal/instrumental style known as rhythm and blues that emerged as another jazz offshoot in the 1940s, well represented by Lionel Hampton and Illinois Jacquet.

must know

By the time Elvis Presley had stamped his own mark on the pop landscape, other musical styles, including country music and electric 'urban' blues, had also inserted themselves into the rock-and-roll mix. But rock's jazz lineage was obvious at its inception.

Seminal rhythm and blues bands

One key figure in launching 'r&b' was alto saxophonist and vocalist Louis Jordan, a Chick Webb alumnus who formed his combo the Tympany Five in 1938. During the war, Jordan's band gained great popularity with a series of novelty hits including 'Ain't Nobody Here but Us Chickens' and 'Caldonia', which emphasized an infectious backbeat and a broad sense of humour rooted in African American culture. Jordan was continuing the ongoing tradition of race recordings, albeit with an inclusive, good-natured spirit that also appealed to mainstream audiences and anticipated the work of rock pioneer Chuck Berry.

At the same time, Nat Cole's urbane trio music was spawning a darker, more blues-based variant in Los Angeles combos like Johnny Moore's Three Blazers, featuring brooding piano and vocals by Charles Brown that influenced the watershed jazz/pop/soul phenomenon Ray Charles. Time would blur the jazz/r&b line further, to the point that Joe Turner could help launch rock through his recordings 'Chains of Love' and 'Shake, Rattle and Roll' in the early 1950s without appreciably altering his original Kansas City style.

Lionel Hampton's rocking big band

A jazz instrumentalist in a big band context gave both r&b and rock great impetus. From the time he organized his own band in 1940, vibist Lionel Hampton dedicated himself to a celebratory (some would say hysterical) good-time music of high energy and a heavy beat. There had been flamboyance in big band music before, but Hampton translated that frenzy into an instrumental context. The exuberance he often displayed when he played drums (his original instrument) and concluded his solos by jumping on the tom-toms was picked up by his entire band.

Hampton's band was anything but one-dimensional, and it gave early exposure to such diverse talents as tenor saxophonist Dexter Gordon, bassist Charles Mingus, guitarist Wes Montgomery, trumpeter Clifford Brown, arranger Quincy Jones and vocalists Dinah Washington, Betty Carter and Little Jimmy Scott.

Still, the definitive Hampton sideman was tenor saxophonist Jean Baptiste Illinois Jacquet, and the definitive Hampton moment was the raucous Jacquet feature 'Flying Home', where riffs and exhortations built to a tremendous crescendo. Its success allowed Jacquet to launch his own career as a featured soloist with the 'Jazz at the Philharmonic' concert package, where his upper-register honking put strains on supposed jazz propriety. Jacquet also led a popular combo where his command of blues and ballads further blurred the boundaries of art and entertainment. He established the pattern for saxophone populists of a more modern persuasion, including Gene Ammons and James Moody.

Lionel Hampton would often leave his vibes and generate excitement with his first instrument, the drums.

must know

Illinois Jacquet's inspired improvisation on the 1942 recording of 'Flying Home' was permanently incorporated into arrangements of the song – and became perhaps the most oft-repeated solo in jazz history.

OPPOSITE: **Louis Jordan helped usher in rhythm and blues with his small group and his humorous vocals.**

Enter the modernists

Jazz was driven even further from the popular mainstream by a new generation of musicians and the innovations they made a part of the basic jazz language. These younger players – including Charlie Parker and Dizzy Gillespie – tended to be virtuoso instrumentalists, schooled in the discipline of the big bands but unwilling to settle for the limited feature space available to orchestra sidemen.

While still favouring the blues and pop song forms as the basis of their improvisations, the new crop of musicians preferred more complex and irregularly accented melodies, more sophisticated harmonic modulations and trip hammer tempos. They sought to expand upon the abstractions of Lester Young and the stream-of-consciousness creativity exemplified when Coleman Hawkins returned from Europe in 1939 and recorded his classic variations on 'Body and Soul'. They shared and refined their individual discoveries in Harlem after-hours clubs like Minton's Playhouse and Monroe's Uptown House. The new music was called bebop, after a Dizzy Gillespie composition that was among the first recorded examples of the style, and its leading exponent was alto saxophonist Charlie Parker.

Charlie Parker's origins

Parker was born in 1920 and grew up in the fertile musical environment of Kansas City. By the time of his initial recordings with Jay McShann's band in 1941, Parker was already displaying a heady new style that merged the virtuosity of Art Tatum's piano, the melodic daring of Lester Young's tenor sax and a blues-rooted intensity that constituted a

Pianist Jay McShann (*far left*) conducts his big band; a young Charlie Parker is the second saxophonist from the left.

class of its own. When Parker began recording under his own name in 1945, he had logged additional big band experience with Earl Hines and Billy Eckstine and had shared ideas with such contemporaries as trumpeter Gillespie, drummer Kenny Clarke and pianist Thelonious Monk.

Through frequent visits to Harlem jam sessions and in his first nightclub appearances on New York's 52nd Street, Parker had created a style for a slightly younger generation of modernists to rally around. This group of first-generation disciples included pianists Earl 'Bud' Powell and Al Haig, trumpeter Miles Davis, trombonist James 'J. J.' Johnson, saxophonist Edward 'Sonny' Stitt and drummer Max Roach. These musicians represented a loose yet identifiable modernist school even before Parker's recording career began in earnest.

Early bebop classics

Dizzy Gillespie began 1945 with 'Bebop' and 'Good Bait', then cut two sessions with Parker that immortalized 'Salt Peanuts', 'Groovin' High' and 'Hot House'. Parker launched his own career as a leader at year's end, on a recording session that

must know

Once the recording ban had ended, bebop was ready to spread its wings. And spread it did, taking flight in 1945 on a series of historic 78s under Gillespie's and Parker's names.

**Bebop's twin fountainheads,
Charlie Parker and Dizzy Gillespie.**

**Pianist/composer Mary Lou
Williams provided encouragement
to the modernists and in turn took
her own music in more ambitious
directions.**

included Davis, Roach and (on piano and trumpet)
Gillespie. It produced two classic blues, 'Billie's
Bounce' and 'Now's the Time', and the virtuosic
variation on 'Cherokee' called 'Ko Ko'.

Few recordings in jazz history proved as influential
and controversial. Unsympathetic veterans questioned
the supposedly thin tones of horn players who had
dispensed with the expressive vibrato of earlier
soloists. Critics attacked the seemingly nervous
accents and dissonant harmonic choices ('We don't
flat our fifths, we drink them', Eddie Condon quipped)
and lamented the difficulty that bebop presented to
dancers. Cab Calloway, Gillespie's old boss, called the
trumpeter's more confounding experiments 'Chinese
music', and Louis Armstrong also attacked the new
style in similar terms. However, not all of the veterans
rejected bebop, or bop, as it came to be called.
Ellington's tenor sax star Ben Webster loved to join the
jam sessions at Minton's; Mary Lou Williams became a
mentor to younger players including Gillespie and
Monk; and the harmonically audacious Hawkins hired
Monk, Davis and other young innovators.

The bebop craze

A new generation of musicians and nondancing listeners, collectively smaller than the audience that sustained the big bands yet equally passionate, rallied to the modern cause. But the artist most clearly identified with bebop was Charlie Parker.

Jazz had initially been out of the mainstream, a music emerging from the minority community that was frequently heard in illicit establishments. After the mass acceptance of the swing bands, listeners responded to bebop's edgy excitement and its sophisticated virtuosity, and they identified with the countercultural trappings that set the style's leading players apart.

The most committed fans lived for each new 78 by Parker and Gillespie, as earlier jazz listeners had devoured the Armstrong Hot Five and Hot Seven recordings and the Count Basie titles with Lester Young. Where the older disciples had copied the slang and mannerisms of Armstrong and Young, the new acolytes became similarly absorbed in bebop. This could result in such relatively benign fads as the passion for goatees and berets that Gillespie triggered. When the mistaken notion that emulating Parker's heroin addiction could lead to Parker-like musical ability gained currency, the hero-worship had a far more destructive effect.

Parker as icon

In his brief and often sensationalized lifetime, and to an even greater extent after his death at age 34 in 1955, Parker became the emblematic bebopper.

did you know?

Bebop restored jazz's reputation for unconventionality, as the new wave of players seemed intent on breaking rules both musical and nonmusical.

did you know?

In both his music and his life, Charlie Parker managed to evoke more passion – both pro and con – than any of his contemporaries.

More clearly removed from previous jazz generations than Gillespie, who still preferred big bands and humorous stage gambits including dancing and scat singing, and less alienating than the inscrutable Monk, Parker had a searing emotional quality to his music that seemed to provide a soundtrack to the drug and alcohol abuse, the erratic behavior and occasional hospitalizations that fuelled his legend. Near the end of his life, Parker lamented that many of those who came to hear him play were only seeking a glimpse of 'the world's greatest junkie, the supreme hipster'. Yet even his most casual fans responded to the visceral intensity in his playing. Together with the more commercial rhythm and blues players (including saxophonist Paul Williams, who turned Parker's 'Now's the Time' into the pop hit 'The Hucklebuck') and such raw 'urban' innovators as Muddy Waters, Parker took the blues into the post-war era.

must know

Charlie Parker's intensity gave jazz, particularly the blues sensibility that is so central to its origins, a contemporary immediacy.

An early example of modern all-stars: (*left to right*) Charlie Parker, Miles Davis, Allen Eager and Kai Winding.

Emergence of the small group

For the majority of the decade in which he reigned as the acknowledged leader of the new style, Parker's working life involved leading a combo, usually a quintet, on recording sessions and in nightclubs. He had played for dancers in the big bands yet found a more natural forum for expressing his new ideas in intimate situations where the focus was on listening. In this sense, the new music dovetailed with the economic realities of the growing number of independent record labels, which often produced recording sessions on limited budgets and couldn't afford to record big bands, and the nightclubs that took the place of ballrooms as the centre of jazz performance.

The Charlie Parker Quintet

Members of the new generation of jazz musicians were not alone in turning their back on big bands, as older virtuoso soloists such as Coleman Hawkins and Lester Young had already anticipated the shift to combo format. Yet for Parker in particular, a configuration like that of his most famous quintet – with Davis, pianist Irving 'Duke' Jordan, bassist Tommy Potter and Roach – proved ideal for expressing speed, technique and the often contrasting personalities within a combo. The trajectory of Parker's New York performing venues as his career progressed – from after-hours Harlem spots to clubs on 52nd Street like Birdland (named in his honour) and finally to Greenwich Village haunts – also traced the route jazz was travelling, from the black community through a more broadly commercial way-station to the precincts of intellectuals.

must know

Bebop reinforced the growing conviction that jazz was an art form, and its practitioners sought venues that were more appropriate for creative expression than the customary ballrooms and dance halls.

must know

The recording Parker's quintet made for the Savoy and Dial labels in 1947–1948 defined bebop – and redefined how jazz ensembles should look and sound.

Parker (*centre left*) in the more familiar confines of his working quintet, with bassist Tommy Potter (*left*), Miles Davis (*centre right*) and an unidentified pianist.

Jazz at the Philharmonic

Parker and fellow musicians such as Ella Fitzgerald and Oscar Peterson were not confined exclusively to the combo and the club. Their reach extended to the concert hall, through a Philharmonic series Norman Granz initiated in 1944, as well as to live jazz recordings.

In addition to several triumphant small-band recordings, key products of Charlie Parker's traumatic first visit to California are the recordings of his live 1946 performances as part of Jazz at the Philharmonic, or JATP as it came to be known. These events were some of the first indications (together with Duke Ellington's annual Carnegie Hall appearances that began in 1943) that jazz could find a home in the more formal settings where symphony orchestras and classical soloists were presented.

Not that JATP concerts were confined to the music's more esoteric aspects. They were organized jam sessions, loose and extroverted and often derided for the tenor sax solos by regulars Illinois Jacquet and Flip Phillips (born Joseph Filipelli) that approached r&b exhibitionism. In honouring Granz's preference for the spontaneous, JATP drove home the point that not all 'serious' music was committed to paper or lacked a sense of celebration. At its best, as in the concert that produced Parker's incredible solo on 'Lady, Be Good', JATP presented informal cross-generational summit encounters where Parker and Gillespie could stand shoulder to shoulder with Young and Hawkins.

Tenor saxophonist Flip Phillips (seen here in a jam session that also included his Woody Herman bandmates Bill Harris on trombone and Chubby Jackson on bass) helped raise the temperature at Jazz at the Philharmonic concerts.

JATP's 1944 debut concert at Hollywood's Philharmonic Auditorium had been recorded, a practice that had its own impact. Edited versions of JATP jams on 12-inch 78s became the first commercially issued live jazz recordings, and their popularity turned the series into an international touring phenomenon.

Ella Fitzgerald

Ella Fitzgerald had abandoned the big band format in 1941, after two years of trying to hold Chick Webb's orchestra together following the drummer's death. Working in front of a trio had led her to a greater emphasis on scat singing. Her improvisations on 'Lady Be Good', 'Flying Home' and 'How High the Moon' were touched by the innovations of the modernists yet possessed a sweet-tempered bravura that sustained Fitzgerald's popularity. After Granz took over her personal management in 1948, her hard-swinging sets became the climactic trademark of JATP presentations.

Oscar Peterson

Pianist Peterson was a black Canadian unknown in the United States when Granz introduced him at a 1949 JATP concert. Peterson merged the breeziness of Nat Cole's early trio playing with the virtuosity and expansiveness of Art Tatum, and he quickly became the workhorse of the JATP enterprise. His own trio, with bassist Ray Brown from the beginning and first a guitarist (Herb Ellis from 1953 to 1958) and then a drummer (Ed Thigpen from 1959 to 1965), quickly became the most frequently recorded jazz group of the period.

Ella Fitzgerald.

Oscar Peterson.

Granz, the record producer

Recorded concert performances made producer Norman Granz an internationally acknowledged jazz impresario. He soon launched his own independent label that operated under the logos Clef, Norgran and Verve. By the time Granz sold the company in 1960, it had become the dominant independent jazz label. A far less positive development during the same period was the growing identification of jazz with drug abuse.

Granz's label managed to get Fitzgerald, Peterson, Parker, Gillespie, Young, Basie, Hawkins, Holiday, Ben Webster and Stan Getz under contract at various points. The jam-session atmosphere Granz loved permeated many of his recorded productions, but he also conceived several concept albums of wide impact. Two of his studio initiatives with Charlie Parker underscore important new contexts for jazz musicians.

The Afro-Cuban influence

In 1949 Parker recorded as the featured guest with Machito's Afro-Cubans, the orchestra led by vocalist Machito (Frank Grillo). Under the musical direction of the multi-instrumentalist Mario Bauza, Machito's band had been the first to successfully merge the rhythms and forms of Afro-Cuban music with big-band jazz concepts. Gillespie, a colleague of Bauza's during their days in Cab Calloway's trumpet section, became the prime champion of the merger when he added the great Cuban conga drummer Chano Pozo (Luciano Pozo y Gonzales) to his own big band in 1947.

must know

Ella Fitzgerald's legendary Songbook series (1956–1964) set the stage for establishing the pantheon of American popular standards.

This promising stylistic conjunction spawned other music, including Stan Kenton's orchestral tribute to Machito and the growing presence of jazz soloists in the ranks of Tito Puente, Tito Rodriguez and other Latin bandleaders. Two popular combos, the quintet pianist George Shearing founded in 1953 and the group formed by his vibist Cal Trader a year later, blurred the lines of demarcation even further.

Jazz with strings

Granz also recorded Parker with strings in 1949 and 1950, fulfilling a lifelong ambition of the saxophonist's and inspiring a small but constant series of similar recordings from instrumentalists with the artistic or commercial clout to warrant such lavish treatment. Parker was extremely proud of his work with strings, especially his stunning interpretation of 'Just Friends', and his string recordings were easily his most popular. To the true bebop believer, however, these and other Granz projects were concessions to mass taste, not to mention a significant cut below the brilliance of Parker in his regular habitat.

The birth of bootleg

Charlie Parker's more intimate performances were also exhaustively documented, since he lived in a period when frequent live broadcasts from nightclubs could be captured by the new technology of disc and tape recorders. Fans made their own copies of radio 'airchecks' as well as concerts, club sets and informal sessions, generating an astounding amount of unauthorized Parker recordings that began surfacing before his death

Machito, with maracas, was the first important Afro-Latin bandleader to touch and be touched by the world of jazz.

Charlie Parker's followers went to great lengths to document his live performances.

and swelled in the ensuing decades. These innumerable versions of the same bebop staples, plus the many alternative takes made available by the labels for which he recorded, testify to Parker's inexhaustible creativity and have yielded several masterpieces, including the 1953 *Jazz at Massey Hall* recordings of a summit meeting in Toronto of Parker, Gillespie, Powell, Roach and Charles Mingus. In their more rough and unpolished form, often with everything other than the alto sax solos omitted to save precious recording material, such clandestine recordings also reinforced Parker's status as a cult figure.

Jazz and drugs

There is no denying that the image of a self-destructive outsider contributed to Parker's aura, and that his heroin dependence in particular helped establish a negative stereotype for his musical generation that took decades to shake. There had been legendary addictive personalities in earlier jazz history, most notably the alcoholic Bix Beiderbecke; and there were previous jazz allusions to controlled substances, most famously in Cab Calloway's 1930s signature 'Minnie the Moocher'. Gene Krupa had served a brief and well-publicized jail sentence on a marijuana charge in 1943.

The identification of jazz and drugs gained force later in the 1940s, as three of the music's leading voices became involved in publicized drug infractions. Lester Young's 1945 sentence to a detention barracks while serving in the army, ostensibly for marijuana possession, was probably the result of institutional racism and Young's

While Cab Calloway was not himself an abuser of drugs, he sang about those who 'kicked the gong around' in his popular sagas featuring Minnie the Moocher.

idiosyncratic and distinctly unmilitary personality. Likewise, Parker's commitment to the Camarillo Sanatorium in California for erratic drug-related behaviour in 1946 and Billie Holiday's imprisonment on heroin charges the following year may have given further evidence of racial double-standards, yet they reflected addictions no less real. While the immediate post-war period saw important gains for the black members of American society, these gains appeared far too incremental for many in a generation that had proven its patriotism during the war years.

Hollywood reinforces the stereotype

Musicians have for a long time complained that the drug problems of jazz stars such as Billie Holiday and Charlie Parker were blown out of all proportion, to the point at which the public assumed that most jazz innovators must be sociopaths. Films over the years have contributed to this image, beginning with Frank Sinatra's portrayal of fictional drummer Frankie Machine in *The Man with the Golden Arm* (1955) and on through the biopics *Lady Sings the Blues* (1972) and *Bird* (1986), on Holiday and Parker, respectively, and the fictional *Round Midnight* (1986), which borrowed well-known incidents from the lives of Young and Bud Powell. While often sensationalized, these films did reflect the significance of substance abuse in the jazz world of the period. The careers of many prominent musicians were interrupted by drug problems in the 1940s and 1950s, and for a significant few, including Parker and Holiday, these addictions would prove fatal.

The sense among the general public that jazz was populated by addictive personalities was fuelled by such films as *The Man with the Golden Arm*.

The Parker of the piano

Despite this situation, an astounding amount of great music was created in the late 1940s, beginning with the players who formed Parker's immediate circle – especially Bud Powell, Tadd Dameron, Thelonious Monk and Lennie Tristano.

must know

Tenor saxophonist Don Byas, drummer Kenny Clarke, bassist Oscar Pettiford and many others saw Europe as a refuge from America's racism and musical indifference during these decades.

Bud Powell, the pianist who best captured the speed and complexity of Parker's alto playing, defined the standard for modern piano in his early trio, solo and quintet recordings. Yet Powell was also an erratic presence. Mental problems, which appear to have been caused by a police beating in 1945, led to lengthy incarcerations, where primitive treatments left Powell more fragile and withdrawn than ever. His brilliant technique suffered, leading Powell and his family to retreat to the more supportive atmosphere of Paris in 1959.

Bud Powell, one of the most brilliant – and unstable – of the era's innovators.

Tadd Dameron and Fats Navarro

Tadd Dameron, who also played piano but is remembered as one of the era's greatest composers, visited Paris when he led a quintet with Miles Davis at the city's historic Jazz Festival of 1949; yet Dameron was fated to suffer and succumb to his addiction at home. During his period of greatest activity in 1947–1949, he led one of the most significant of the early modern groups at the Royal Roost on 52nd Street in Manhattan. Dameron's band featured trumpeter Theodore 'Fats' Navarro, whose melodic gifts and balanced technique were easier for other trumpeters to grasp than the more virtuosic convolutions of Gillespie, and whose primary impact before his 1950 death came from a series of recordings with Dameron and Powell.

The high priest of bebop

A third important pianist/composer had mentored Powell and collaborated actively with Parker and Gillespie in defining the modern jazz vocabulary. It took far longer, though, for the public and even many musicians to see beyond Thelonious Monk's personal idiosyncrasies and hear through his dissonant, rhythmically unpredictable creations.

More clearly than any of his contemporaries, Monk, garbed in dark glasses and a variety of unusual hats and given to rare and frequently cryptic pronouncements, was a man ahead of his time. From his first recordings as a bandleader in 1947 until he began his influential tenure on the Riverside label eight years later, he was valued more for his quirky yet undeniably fascinating writing than for his percussive and often jarring playing. It did not help

must know

Billed as the 'High Priest of Bebop', Thelonious Monk was the quintessential jazz eccentric.

that Monk, one musician without a dependence on narcotics, refused to offer evidence against a friend and as a result lost his cabaret card, the licence performers were required to hold if they wished to work steadily in New York City establishments where alcohol was served. For years, Monk did most of his playing on a piano in the kitchen of his Manhattan apartment, where young musicians including pianist Randy Weston and tenor saxophonist Theodore 'Sonny' Rollins received intensive tutorials.

Monk's time arrived after Riverside recorded him in a variety of contexts that emphasized his brilliance as a pianist, composer and bandleader, and after the reinstatement of his cabaret card led to an extended 1957 stay at the Five Spot. At this Greenwich Village nightclub the Monk quartet – featuring John Coltrane – was hailed as the most exciting sound to hit jazz since Parker's and Gillespie's collaborations a dozen years earlier.

The first jazz progressive

Lennie Tristano, another pianist and leader often considered as far out as Monk, had a more immediate impact. Before arriving in New York from his native Chicago, Tristano developed a personal philosophy of improvisation and attracted the first of what would become a significant number of students. The style was captured in a series of 1949 recordings with his two leading disciples, alto saxophonist Lee Konitz and tenor saxophonist Warne Marsh. While Tristano's influence was felt, particularly after Konitz became a model for several European musicians, it might have had a broader impact had the pianist not devoted his primary focus to teaching after 1951.

did you know?

Lennie Tristano's 'Intuition' was totally improvised and eventually was viewed as a harbinger of the free jazz movement that emerged a decade later.

At the height of his popularity in 1950, no one was considered more 'far out' than pianist Lennie Tristano.

Tristano learned classic recorded performances by ear. He then eliminated tonal inflection and rhythmically active accompaniment in favour of unfettered melodic invention. The systematic air surrounding Tristano's music made it appear that he was proposing a more intellectual or 'progressive' alternative to bebop. With perspective, however, Tristano can be seen as one of Parker's most individual students, and the creator of a music that could not have existed without bebop and the harmonically astute Art Tatum as primary sources.

Bebop branches out

Two styles with a bebop foundation encompass much of the best jazz of the 1950s – cool jazz ('West Coast' jazz) and hard bop ('East Coast' jazz). It's hard to identify a young musician from the period who was not working in these or other variations on bebop.

must know

'Cool' was considered the domain of white musicians. Yet Miles Davis, whose recordings mark the birth of cool, was black – and the ensemble that most successfully immersed itself in European influences, the Modern Jazz Quartet, consisted of four African Americans.

Possible exceptions were pianist Erroll Garner, cornetist Reuben 'Ruby' Braff and clarinetist Bob Wilber. Garner did record with Parker once, but he rose to enormous popularity with a totally personal merger of swing and more modern elements. Braff and Wilber were representative of the occasional throwbacks who played exclusively with more traditional older stylists.

Elements of the cool style

As it grew into a marketable commodity, cool jazz became identified with lighter, vibrato-free lines, the use of instruments (including French horn, tuba, flute and oboe) more familiar from classical music than earlier jazz, and a greater emphasis on counterpoint and other supposedly 'classical' techniques. While the style became identified with California, many of its leading lights, including saxophonists Stan Getz and Gerry Mulligan and trumpeter Milton 'Shorty' Rogers, were from the East Coast. While cool jazz did reflect responses to a diversity of influences, it was also rooted in the Kansas City continuum of Basie, Young and Parker.

The light, floating sonic palette of cool jazz had originally surfaced in the dance orchestra led by pianist Claude Thornhill that employed French horns, tuba and various woodwinds in addition to the more typical big band instruments. Gil Evans, who became Thornhill's primary arranger in 1941, was fascinated by the colours these instruments placed at his disposal and employed them for a range of impressionistic tonal effects while simultaneously embracing the new sounds of modern small groups. In 1947 Evans orchestrated Parker's 'Yardbird Suite' and 'Donna Lee', the Parker/Gillespie collaboration 'Anthropology' and Illinois Jacquet's hit 'Robbins' Nest' for Thornhill – often as features for the band's distinctive new alto saxophone soloist Lee Konitz.

Evans also began to share his ideas with young musicians from the Parker quintet orbit such as Miles Davis and pianist John Lewis. Their discussions, which also included the young arranger and baritone saxophonist Gerry Mulligan, led to the short-lived but seminal Miles Davis Nonet, a compact version of the Thornhill band featuring Davis, Konitz and Mulligan as soloists and the innovative writing of Evans, Lewis and Mulligan.

Gerry Mulligan (*left*) and his baritone sax became emblematic of the new sounds from California (tenor saxophonist John 'Zoot' Sims is at right).

Pianist Claude Thornhill leads the band often credited as the harbinger of the cool style – note the presence of two French horns.

A young Shorty Rogers, before he acquired his trademark goatee.

Reverberations west

While the Davis Nonet obtained only one booking, it did manage to record on three different occasions between 1949 and 1950. These titles, later dubbed the *Birth of the Cool*, had a powerful impact, most directly on the work of Shorty Rogers, a young trumpeter and arranger who made similar use of low brass voices in the recordings of his Giants that began to appear in 1951. Rogers also drew heavily on the riff-based example of the Count Basie band and, like scores of tenor saxophonists at the time, the surface restraint of Basie's former star soloist Lester Young. The 'cool' that Rogers came to exemplify thus echoed jazz's hotter climes, as did the playing of a favourite Rogers collaborator, alto saxophonist Art Pepper.

Hollywood embraces the cool

Like many other former big band sidemen adjusting to post-war shifts in the music industry, Rogers found a new outlet for his music in Hollywood studios, where the music for films and television took on a distinct jazz flavour. While the racial discrimination that prevailed in Hollywood studios goes far in explaining the predominance of white jazz musicians in California, black veterans such as Benny Carter and Harry 'Sweets' Edison also quietly cracked barriers in the segregated system.

Harry 'Sweets' Edison left the Count Basie band to become one of the first African American musicians who was a mainstay of the Hollywood recording studios.

Small group sans piano

Not all of the musicians who ventured west were interested in studio work. Gerry Mulligan relocated to Los Angeles while writing for Stan Kenton's band and formed a quartet for appearances at a nightclub called The Haig. In this band, Mulligan's deep yet mobile baritone sax was paired with the fragile and unimpeachably lyrical trumpet of Chet Baker, a self-taught newcomer who had previously impressed no less a figure than Parker. The pair improvised simultaneously, a practice that harkened back to New Orleans yet took on a thoroughly modern veneer through the absence of piano in the rhythm section. Mulligan's lean, witty quartet sound, as definitive of West Coast cool as that of any band's, became instantly popular and turned both the leader and Baker into stars.

As the decade progressed, Mulligan proved himself unwilling to confine himself geographically or stylistically and managed to perform and record with an astonishing number of jazz greats of the current and earlier eras. He applied his loose quartet approach to his Concert Jazz Band, which he formed in New York in 1960. Baker, who added vulnerable vocals to his arsenal shortly after leaving Mulligan's group in 1953, also came east and then relocated to Europe when his hopes for movie stardom were sidetracked by drug problems.

More western sounds

Some of the new sounds emerging from the West Coast were actually created by westerners. Saxophonist and clarinetist Jimmy Giuffre, a Texan, studied advanced compositional techniques in southern California and applied them as well as his affinity for folk music themes in his intimate Jimmy Giuffre 3. That band eliminated drums and – in one unusual reed/trombone/guitar configuration – bass. The quietly original guitarist Jim Hall had joined Giuffre after his 1955 debut with Foreststorn 'Chico'

There is a drum set in the picture, but the Jimmy Giuffre 3 (pictured here with the leader on clarinet and guitarist Jim Hall) was influential for its omission of percussion.

One of the true West Coast musicians, California native Chico Hamilton.

Hamilton, a black Los Angeles native who played in Mulligan's quartet before creating a band that featured flute and cello and placed great emphasis on the leader's atmospheric percussion.

Enter Dave Brubeck

By far the most popular musician to emerge from California was pianist Dave Brubeck, a product of studies with composer Darius Mihaud as well as his own experiments in counterpoint and atonality with like-minded contemporaries in the San Francisco area. Brubeck's early octet proved too esoteric for popular tastes, but his recordings in a trio setting planted the seed of a mass following that blossomed after alto saxophonist Paul Desmond was added to the group. The contrast between Desmond's limpid elegance and Brubeck's weightier complexities, and the conversational improvisations that the pair generated, bore an intellectual appeal for those who now approached jazz as a more purely listening experience.

With an uncanny sense of where both the technology and the audience was headed, Brubeck took advantage of the new 33 1/3 rpm 'long-playing' records, which initially held three to four times more music than the still-standard 78 singles. After recording and releasing several of the quartet's nightclub performances, Brubeck began obtaining bookings on college campuses, which were recorded and released commercially as well. Brubeck continued to build throughout the decade, and in 1960 the quartet's album *Time Out*, among the first examples of jazz performed in meters such as 5/4 and 9/8, brought jazz into the realm of million-selling pop singles via Paul Desmond's composition 'Take Five'.

did you know?

By 1954 Dave Brubeck was so popular that he was featured on the cover of *Time* magazine.

The MJQ

The Modern Jazz Quartet made many of the same inroads with college and concert hall audiences from its base in New York. The MJQ originated as a performing unit when its members, who were the rhythm section of Dizzy Gillespie's 1946 big band, began cultivating a veneer of chamber-music propriety when they first reunited in the early 1950s. Yet the jazz achievements of MJQ members could not be denied. Vibist Milt Jackson was one of the jazz's most exceptional blues and ballad performers, and pianist John Lewis had worked extensively with Charlie Parker, Lester Young and Dizzy Gillespie. The band's original rhythm team consisted of bassist Ray Brown and drummer Kenny Clarke; Percy Heath replaced Brown in 1952 and Connie Kay took Clarke's chair in 1955, fixing the personnel of one of the period's most artistically and commercially successful ensembles.

The Modern Jazz Quartet (*left to right*: **John Lewis, Percy Heath, Connie Kay and Milt Jackson) in what for them was relatively informal attire.**

A harder alternative

Alternatives to cool jazz were inevitable, especially from the contingent of young black players remaining on the East Coast. Uninterested as a rule in big band work, and still awaiting colour-blind opportunities in radio and television orchestras and theatre pit bands, musicians such as Max Roach, Art Blakey and especially Miles Davis developed a more aggressive and edgy hard bop sound.

Max Roach was among the modern drummers who shifted the orientation of the music in the early 1950s.

Focus on percussion

The examples of Charlie Parker and Lester Young were directly manifest in the style's emphasis on extended solos based on the blues and popular song forms. But it was the more prominent contributions of drummers that set hard bop apart from the music of the previous decade. Max Roach and Art Blakey, two of the definitive drummers of the period, led their own successful bands while also recording frequently in support of other leaders. Together with other drummers who worked primarily as sidemen in the period, including Joseph 'Philly Joe' Jones and Roy Haynes, Roach and Blakey created a new equilibrium in the small group that encouraged more interactive accompaniment from pianists as well as a heated fluency from trumpet and saxophone players.

Groups such as the quintet led by Roach and trumpeter Clifford Brown, the various editions of Art Blakey's Jazz Messengers, and the studio and touring combos of Miles Davis refreshed the ensemble possibilities of bebop with new compositions and subtle arrangements that made the most of five or six voices. But hard bop's primary action was in the sustained groove of the now-extended solos.

Larger and slower 'long-playing' 33⅓ rpm records, introduced in 1948 as 10-inch discs carrying roughly 12 minutes of music per side, were quickly supplanted by the 12-inch, 20-minute-per-side version in 1955, but the smaller format lasted long enough for Miles Davis, already moving beyond the narrow confines of his Nonet's 78s, to learn how to productively stretch out on long-play. Davis developed a vivid trumpet sound that traded the technical brilliance of his idol Gillespie and former boss Parker for the intimacy of a Sinatra. He also had impeccable taste in musical associates, made dramatic use of silence and space, and reduced the usual emphasis on crowded harmonic motion. Davis thus was able to seize quickly upon the potential of the new album formats. His various all-star bands of contrasting, like-minded players produced informal yet memorable LPs – albums such as *Dig* and *Walkin'* that defined the modern 'blowing session' while exposing such young stars as tenor saxophonist Sonny Rollins and pianist Horace Silver.

The first great Miles Davis Quintet

Davis also overcame his heroin addiction earlier than many of his peers. By 1955 his renewed health and success in the recording studio led him to assemble a remarkable working band – with tenor saxophonist John Coltrane, pianist William 'Red' Garland, bassist Paul Chambers and drummer Philly Joe Jones – that was unsurpassed in both hard swinging and dramatic balladry.

Hazards of the jazz life

The limited cachet of cool jazz, not to mention the general acceptance of big band swing, eluded many

of the musicians who became associated with hard bop. The
diminishing number of venues where such uncompromising
music could be performed also contributed to making the style
a distinctly non-mainstream music. What came to be known
euphemistically as 'personal problems' interrupted or
prematurely concluded several promising careers, while more
mundane hazards of the touring life claimed others. No loss
was more shocking than that of the clean-living Clifford Brown,
a young trumpeter with a personality on the horn to rival
Davis's and far more technique. Brown became a star in the
quintet he formed with Max Roach in 1954 and then was killed
in a highway accident while en route to a performance two
years later at the age of 25. Roach carried on with sidemen such
as Sonny Rollins, an ingenious master of sustained

**Clifford Brown displayed amazing
progress and influence in his
tragically brief career.**

improvisations filled with caustic humour. Rollins already had built the foundations of his growing reputation by working with Monk and Davis before blending with Brown in the Brown/Roach Quintet shortly before the trumpeter's death.

Both tenor saxophonist **Sonny Rollins** (*left*) and pianist **Horace Silver** (*right*) benefited from early exposure with Miles Davis before becoming style setters themselves in the mid-1950s.

Enter the funk

Another important drummer-led band of the era was the Jazz Messengers, a unit originally conceived as a cooperative quintet that was driven by the volcanic surges of Art Blakey and the slick writing and piano of Horace Silver. In 1956 Silver left the Messengers to form his own intensely swinging quintet. Blakey proceeded to recruit more talented and still-unsung new starts including saxophonists Jackie McLean, Johnny Griffin, Benny Golson and Wayne Shorter, trumpeter Lee Morgan and pianist Bobby Timmons. In the style set by Silver, many of the new Messengers also contributed compositions drenched in blues and gospel inflection. 'Funky' and 'soulful' became favourite adjectives for describing the growing infusion of church music fervour that marked the output of Silver, Blakey and other bandleaders such as alto saxophonist Julian 'Cannonball' Adderley.

Getting back to rhythm and blues

At this point hard bop touched upon the more bluesy and populist styles of players such as Gene Ammons and James Moody, as well as the wide-ranging influence of vocalist Ray Charles and his jazz-rooted supporting band. Informal recordings and Dizzy Gillespie's big band added spark to the mid-1950s' jazz scene.

Jazz's link to black church music could be heard in groups built around the Hammond B-3 organ, an instrument that gained instant popularity after Jimmy Smith began recording in 1956. Smith's stunning dexterity with twin keyboards and bass pedals brought the instrument into the modern era, with the organ's dynamic properties often suggesting a shouting big band.

Jamming in the studio

Some of the most memorable jazz in this period was created on informal recording sessions under the names of star sidemen like Rollins and John Coltrane, another tenor saxophonist who spent valuable time in the employ of Davis and Monk. These players and several lesser personalities were satisfying the demand for music to fill the recording industry's new album format. Leading the way were independent labels, including Blue Note, Prestige, Riverside and Savoy in New York, Argo and Vee-Jay in Chicago, and Contemporary, Fantasy and Pacific Jazz in California.

The constant activity of the East Coast labels made the converted living room that served as a studio for definitive jazz recording engineer Rudy Van Gelder as

must know

In nightclubs catering to a working-class black clientele, bands consisting of tenor sax, organ, guitar and drums became the norm, playing music that merged bebop, r&b and gospel.

famous as the stages of Birdland or the Village Vanguard. A few of the albums, including Rollins's *Saxophone Colossus* and *Way Out West* and Coltrane's *Blue Train* and *Giant Steps*, quickly attained masterpiece status. Other, less charismatic voices, like that of saxophonist Hank Mobley, the definitive journeyman (Roach, Gillespie, Blakey, Silver and Davis all appear on his résumé) who led bands primarily in Van Gelder's studio, would not live long enough to see their albums declared classics decades later.

Gillespie's modern big band

Modern jazz also had an impact on the diminished big band scene, even though the odds of keeping a large ensemble on the road after World War II were long indeed. Gillespie continued to find the format best suited to his outgoing personality and brashly complex horn playing, and he laboured valiantly to maintain an orchestra on more than one occasion. His big band of 1946–1950 proved through such tours de force as 'Things to Come' and 'Cool Breeze' that bebop could be created on the canvas of larger ensembles, while 'Manteca' and 'Cubano Be, Cubano Bop' announced the seeds of the jazz/Afro-Cuban merger. After several years of leading small groups and participating in JATP tours, Gillespie organized a new big band in 1956 that featured bright young writers including Quincy Jones and Benny Golson.

Much of the new Gillespie band's work took place on foreign tours of South America and the Middle East sponsored by the U.S. State Department. At this time, Voice of America disc jockey Willis Conover became a major presence in Iron Curtain countries, where listeners tuned in to his jazz programmes clandestinely.

OPPOSITE: **In addition to the influential vocals of Ray Charles, the piano and arranging on his early recordings underscored the ongoing link between jazz and blues.**

Dizzy Gillespie in a photo taken before someone sat on his horn in 1953 and inspired him to switch to a trumpet with an upturned bell.

must know

Dizzy Gillespie's State Department-sponsored tours were among the first formal acknowledgements of jazz's value as an international symbol of American culture.

Big band survivors

Bandleaders Woody Herman and Stan Kenton – with roots in the Swing Era plus an affinity for newer sounds – were among those able to keep orchestras afloat through much of the 1940s and 1950s.

Woody Herman made the transition from swing to modern jazz, helping to set new orchestral standards in the process.

Woody Herman's Herds

The relatively self-effacing clarinet soloist Woodrow 'Woody' Herman had led an orchestra since taking over the Isham Jones band in 1936. He enjoyed a modest early success leading what was known as 'the band that plays the blues', then underwent a modernist conversion during World War II that was evidenced in dynamic 1945 recordings by what was now called the Herman Herd. Yet even with star soloists including trombonist Bill Harris and tenor saxophonist Joe 'Flip' Phillips, and the inspired Ellington-influenced writing of Ralph Burns and Neal Hefti, Herman succumbed to the economic downturn of 1946 and disbanded.

Herman returned a year later with his Second Herd, a unit that made its allegiance to Lester Young's and Charlie Parker's style of modernism even clearer than its predecessor through a distinctive blend of three tenors and one baritone sax. Stan Getz, John 'Zoot' Sims, Al Cohn and Gene Ammons all played tenors against Serge Chaloff's baritone in the Second Herd before Herman disbanded again, only to form a Third Herd that managed to work more often than not throughout the 1950s.

Easily the most successful of Herman's sidemen was Getz, who used the forum of the Second Herd as a platform for his pure sound and quietly emotional style. After leaving Herman, Getz would work in a series of small groups, becoming one of the most consistent and popular instrumentalists of the 1950s when not sidetracked by drug and alcohol problems.

Controversial Stan Kenton

Like Herman, Stan Kenton had several financial reversals yet put his stamp on the period with his controversial ensembles. When his bandleading career began in 1941, Kenton used the Jimmie Lunceford Orchestra as a model and created music for dancers. By 1946 he was describing his music as 'progressive' and moving in an experimental direction. Strengths of this band were the orchestral use of Eddie Safranski's bass and the astounding mobility of a trombone section led by Kai Winding. But these strong points were often overwhelmed by pretence, a problem that continued when Kenton returned from retirement in 1950 with an Innovations in Modern Music orchestra. This group included a string section of 16 musicians that performed such extended compositions as Bob Graettinger's futuristic 'City of Glass'. Kenton spent the rest of the decade veering between similarly ambitious projects and a greater emphasis on swing and strong soloists, with occasional forays into the Latin realm.

There was little middle ground surrounding a musician who many worshipped and an equally vocal number loathed – he was either God or Kent Standum, as a witticism of the day had it. But even the naysayers had to credit that Kenton's recordings contained a healthy amount of superior jazz, especially when Bill Russo and Bill Holman wrote the arrangements and soloists such as trombonist Frank Rosolino and saxophonists Konitz, Sims and Art Pepper received featured space.

In his grander moments, Kenton proved less progressive than the more soft-spoken Gil Evans, who renewed his partnership with Miles Davis in three brilliant concept albums with studio orchestras, *Miles Ahead* (1957), *Porgy and Bess* (1958) and *Sketches of Spain* (1960), or composers such as John Lewis, J. J. Johnson and George Russell. Their occasional studio projects featured advanced compositional elements in a style that attempted to merge the classical and jazz traditions and came to be called Third Stream.

The orchestral vision of bandleader Stan Kenton made him a lightning rod for debates over the music's future.

Gil Evans took the large jazz ensemble in new directions as well, albeit in a more introverted voice.

Rising beyond nostalgia

A good number of the remaining big bands survived on the nostalgia that had already surrounded the Swing Era. Some of the most successful commercially were ghost bands, including the Glenn Miller Orchestra, or various units formed to honour Tommy and Jimmy Dorsey. Count Basie's and Duke Ellington's orchestras were the two bands that remained important creative forces during this period.

must know

The achievements of the Basie and Ellington orchestras in the 1940s and 1950s were key to establishing their status among the leading ensembles in jazz history.

Basie in transition

Count Basie's band remained emblematic of swinging informality throughout the 1940s, building its personality around the leader's cryptic piano, the infectious work of the rhythm section and notable musicians. A parade of tenor saxophonists followed Lester Young's departure in 1940, including Don Byas, Illinois Jacquet, Eli 'Lucky' Thompson and Paul Gonsalves. Trumpeters

Count Basie on stage *circa* 1950, at a time when the decline of big bands forced him briefly to lead a combo.

When Count Basie formed his New Testament Band, arrangers Neal Hefti (*left*) and Ernie Wilkins (*right*) made key contributions to the group's evolving sound.

Buck Clayton and Sweets Edison and trombonists Dickey Wells, Vic Dickenson and J. J. Johnson rounded out the group of notables.

At the same time, a gradual shift to a greater reliance on written arrangements was taking place. After suffering his own business reversals and downsizing to a sextet in 1950, Basie organized a new orchestra in 1952 with a distinctly new personality. The band executed lean yet dynamically extravagant arrangements by Ernie Wilkins, Neal Hefti and others.

The Basie band of the 1950s became known as the New Testament Basie Band. The band could explode – so infectiously on its trademark

did you know?

The New Testament Band was dubbed the 'Atomic Basie band' after releasing its $e=mc^2$ album, which featured a mushroom cloud on the cover.

arrangement of 'April in Paris' that the leader was heard to call for the shout chorus to be repeated 'one more time'. It could purr – as on the seductive 'Li'l Darlin''. And it could most definitely still play the blues – to greatest commercial effect behind the vocals of Joe Williams. By the time the popular Williams left in 1960 to work on his own, it was clear that Basie had created a second band for the ages.

Ellington in concert

Duke Ellington's achievement was more uninterrupted, in terms of activity if not always output. In the three years leading up to the recording ban of 1942, the Ellington Orchestra had produced a string of masterpieces that remain unsurpassed as jazz in a large ensemble setting. 'Ko-Ko', 'Concerto for Cootie', 'Harlem Air Shaft', 'All Too Soon', 'Take the "A" Train' and 'Main Stem' do not begin to exhaust the list of early 1940s Ellington triumphs. These were supplemented by an equally inspired series of small band recordings, often under the titular leadership of star Ellington soloists Johnny Hodges, Rex Stewart and Barney Bigard.

In 1943 Ellington also began an annual series of concerts at Carnegie Hall that provided the opportunity to add extended compositions including 'Black, Brown and Beige' (described by the composer as a 'Tone Parallel to the History of the Negro in America') to his growing body of three-minute miracles. It is unfortunate that studio recordings only incompletely documented many of these longer efforts.

Ellington made other attempts to break compositional ground during the war years with the theatrical revue *Jump for Joy*, which ran in Los Angeles but never reached Broadway. While his larger projects rarely attained commercial success, Ellington continued to rely on his talent for writing hit songs, including 'I Got It Bad (and That Ain't Good)' and 'Don't Get Around Much Anymore'. Even in the relatively lean decade of 1945–1955, when his output was less rewarding, business was at a new low and key sidemen had left his employ, Ellington kept a band together, rebuilding with new stars including trumpeter Clark Terry, tenor saxophonist Paul Gonsalves and drummers Louie Bellson and Sam Woodyard.

Paul Gonsalves's extended Newport solo put Duke Ellington back on top of the big band scene.

A new phenomenon reverses Ellington's fortunes

Two significant events in 1956 changed Ellington's fortunes. Johnny Hodges, the major star soloist of Ellington's first quarter-century as a bandleader, returned to the fold after five years at the head of his own group; and an extravagant extended Gonsalves solo on 'Diminuendo and Crescendo in Blue' at the Newport Jazz Festival caused a near riot.

Newport's image as one mammoth jazz party took hold quickly, and Ellington's appearance at the third annual edition of the event put Newport over the top. Within weeks, Ellington was on the cover of *Time* magazine, and by the time a live recording of his Newport performance was released, he had regained his status as jazz's ultimate composer/bandleader. In the process, the festival phenomenon also earned a permanent niche on the jazz landscape.

did you know?

Jazz owes its 1954 debut in Newport to George Wein, a Boston nightclub owner who was hired to organize concerts that would replace the Rhode Island resort community's failed summer series of classical music.

Celebrating the sources

Ellington's was not the first jazz revival, for the notion of a second life for early styles and older musicians had grown fairly common in the more traditional realms of the music.

Bunk Johnson found himself in the unlikely role of traditional jazz saviour in his final years.

During a 1939 trip to New Orleans, early jazz historians Frederic Ramsey and William Russell discovered 50-year-old retired and still-unrecorded trumpeter Willie 'Bunk' Johnson, a favourite of the young Louis Armstrong. By 1942 Johnson was playing again and recording. The substantial discography Johnson created in the years before his death in 1949 reveals much of the idolatry pinned on him to be wishful projection, as the trumpeter had clearly seen his best days decades earlier. Yet Johnson brought the early New Orleans style back into the public consciousness, with the assistance of such other hometown veterans as trombonist Kid Ory, who worked extensively on the West Coast, and clarinetist George Lewis, who assumed the revivalist mantle at Johnson's death and went on to lead his own successful band throughout the world.

The new revivalists

During the years of Johnson's resurgence, a group of young white musicians in San Francisco working as the Yerba Buena Jazz Band under the direction of trumpeter Lucious 'Lu' Watters was taking a more studied and comprehensive approach to reviving the New Orleans repertoire. Confining itself primarily to both the compositions and the techniques of the earliest players, the Watters band and offshoots formed in later years by two Yerba Buena alumni, trombonist Melvin 'Turk' Murphy and trumpeter Bob Scobey, set the standard for a revival movement that quickly became a worldwide phenomenon. Unfortunately, many of the young traditionalists lacked both the skill and the taste of the Yerba Buenans and the sidemen in Bob Crosby's big band. The latter anticipated the New Orleans revival in the late 1930s in the Bobcats combo and sustained their careers in smaller traditional units after World War II.

Drawing stylistic lines

Proponents of modern jazz often disparaged the traditionalists, damning both players and fans of the New Orleans renaissance as 'mouldy figs'. For them, the term 'Dixieland', the common name for the new style, simply meant an inauthentic imitation of black New Orleans jazz played primarily by white amateurs. Press accounts often reduced the growing diversity of jazz styles to clashes between the 'new' and the 'trad'. As a result, listeners with a diminishing appreciation of jazz's already-rich history began to demand that musicians playing in a style that predated bebop include such traditional warhorses as 'When the Saints Go Marching In' in their repertoire.

Black musicians were not alone in resenting the stereotyping. Eddie Condon tried to distance the revival-mongering by referring to the music he and his associates made as 'Nicksiland', after the club Nick's in Greenwich Village where they performed before Condon opened his own room off Washington Square in 1945. Even such highly sophisticated veterans as Coleman Hawkins and Roy Eldridge often found themselves expected to serve up corny Dixieland fare.

Lu Watters (*left*) gives directions to the members of his Yerba Buena Jazz Band, the first of the successful revivalist units.

Trumpeter Roy Eldridge was among the innovators of the 1930s who found themselves victimized by the traditional/modern schism of the following decade.

Armstrong the all-star

Louis Armstrong, whose studio groups had announced a more modern jazz epoch 20 years earlier, abandoned his big band in 1947 and returned to a combo format. His All Stars groups became a home for other displaced veterans. Musicians in these groups included trombonists Jack Teagarden and Trummy Young, clarinetists Barney Bigard and Edmond Hall and pianist Earl Hines.

must know

His All Star groups helped to cement Louis Armstrong's eminence as an international symbol of America and a constantly touring goodwill ambassador.

After more than a decade at the helm of a big band, Louis Armstrong retrenched with the help of such All Stars as trombonist Jack Teagarden and clarinetist Barney Bigard.

While his band's concert presentation grew predictable, and his ebullient stage manner led some to dismiss him as old fashioned at best or an Uncle Tom at worst, Armstrong continued to sing and play eloquently during the period, producing album-length tributes to Fats Waller and W. C. Handy as well as a surprisingly successful musical retrospective, *Autobiography*, that re-created many of his own early classics. He also recorded new pop material, including early hit versions of 'Blueberry Hill' and 'Mack the Knife'. These successes, as well as frequent appearances on television and in films, made Armstrong familiar (albeit more as an entertainer than an innovative musical artist) to a new generation.

La belle Bechet

Sidney Bechet, whose career had never taken off like Armstrong's, did not begin to extensively document his soprano sax and clarinet on recordings until 1940. Bechet was frustrated with his fortunes in America. After being celebrated when he visited Paris as the star of the city's historic 1949 jazz festival, he was inspired to relocate to France. Back in a country where his music had been embraced in the 1920s, he lived the final decade of his life as a national hero. He has been most widely remembered since his death in 1959 by a statue in Antibes, France, and by his popular recording 'Petite Fleur', which remained a jukebox staple throughout Europe decades later.

The mainstream slump

Circumstances were generally less gratifying for swing-era veterans previously sustained by big band work. At best, they could play in JATP concert settings or in other small groups that featured 'mainstream jazz'. Too often, the likes of Hawkins, Eldridge, Ben Webster and Charlie Shavers found themselves reduced to quasi-Dixieland ensembles or tours as 'singles' on which they played with rhythm sections of varying quality as they travelled from town to town.

Through it all, many of the mainstream musicians continued to thrive musically. Recordings by Hawkins throughout these decades, and Webster in the later part of the period, contain some of their finest music. Lester Young and Billie Holiday made several classic recordings as well, but the physical and psychological suffering each endured took its toll. Despite the contrary claims of fans who heard brilliance in the pathos of their later work, many of the pair's final efforts suggested the unravelling of genius.

This image of a diminished Holiday and Young was made permanent on the 1957 television programme *The Sound of Jazz*, a landmark conclave of giants where both singer and saxophonist made contributions of ravaged eloquence while seemingly struggling to avoid expiring on camera. Neither could sustain the fight for long. Young died in March 1959. Holiday met her end in a hospital bed four months later.

Ben Webster was among those considered old fashioned as bebop became established.

Looking to the future

The passing of jazz giants Parker, Bechet, Holiday and Young imposed a sense of mortality on the jazz world that the still-young music previously had not confronted quite so directly. But more open-minded listeners retained their optimism, given the array of experimenters who had emerged by 1960 and promised an even more exciting future.

Charles Mingus dazzled with his bass playing and his innovative approach to composing and to leading a band.

One man's workshop

Charles Mingus, a virtuoso bassist and ambitious composer, had already established his Jazz Workshop band as a major force by the end of the 1950s. The Workshop, founded in 1955 after Mingus had participated in composer collectives and other experimental ventures, created music of raw emotion that was learned by ear and modified on the spot through Mingus's vocal cues and the freedom provided to each player. Mingus employed 'open form', where song choruses with modulating harmonies were replaced by harmonically static passages of indeterminate length. He also encouraged his horn players to create vocal effects and to merge in chaos-courting passages of collective improvisation.

Working with loyal band members including trombonist Jimmy Knepper and drummer Dannie Richmond instead of established stars, Mingus turned his band into both a musical cauldron and a soapbox for social commentary. 'Fables of Faubus' appeared on his most popular and diverse album, *Mingus Ah Um*, although Columbia Records would not allow 'Faubus' to include the minstrel-like vocal part that Mingus employed in live performances. The 'original' version would appear a year later, when *Mingus Presents Mingus* featuring woodwind innovator Eric Dolphy was recorded for the independent Candid label.

Cecil Taylor's revolution

Mingus was still accepted as part of the jazz continuum – he had, after all, worked with Armstrong, Hampton and Ellington, and been the bassist at the Massey Hall summit meeting of Gillespie, Parker, Powell and Roach. More questions were raised regarding the musical lineage of Cecil Taylor, a pianist/composer who studied at the New England Conservatory and held only brief jobs with Johnny Hodges and Oran 'Hot Lips' Page before forming his own quartet in 1955.

ABOVE: Pianist Cecil Taylor would lead the coming re-evaluation of rhythm, structure and ensemble interaction in jazz.

LEFT: Trombonist Jimmy Knepper is among the important alumni of the Mingus Jazz Workshop.

Taylor began by imposing sophisticated harmonies and rhythms on what remained fairly discernible song forms. Yet it was not long before the abstractions in his music began to obliterate any familiar source points. By 1960, poised to make his final break with jazz convention, Taylor had grown used to being dismissed as an angrier Brubeck on a misguided quest to impose European avant-garde techniques on American music. If his efforts had achieved nothing else, they had introduced the sound of the soprano saxophone into the modern jazz context.

Coleman cuts the chords

The greatest controversy over new jazz directions was created by a musician with far more obvious ties to the blues and swing rhythms. Alto saxophonist Ornette Coleman, a native of Fort Worth, Texas, had gained experience playing r&b as well as bebop when he moved to Los Angeles in the early 1950s and began to develop his own radical approach. Coleman felt that freedom could be gained by dispensing with the chord changes that provided the guideposts for jazz improvisers. The melodies that he wrote were intriguing and almost boppish, but once they had been stated, he and his musicians were free to create variations in an open harmonic field where modulations were realized on the spur of the moment. As the years passed, Coleman found musicians who could work comfortably with his concepts, including trumpeters Don Cherry and Bobby Bradford, bassists Charlie Haden and Scott LaFaro and drummers Ed Blackwell and Billy Higgins.

Coleman's first two albums, for the Los Angeles Contemporary label in 1958 and 1959, proposed a

A white plastic alto saxophone was not the only thing that set Ornette Coleman's music apart.

radical change of jazz's rules. His third recording, *The Shape of Jazz to Come*, for New York's Atlantic Records, seemed to be a manifesto of new freedom. Lines were drawn when the Coleman quartet with Cherry, Haden and Higgins came east to make its New York debut and celebrate the release. Many lovers of bebop and its diverse offshoots received the band's raw, loose and impulsive music as a slap in the face. In fact, Coleman was alternatively attacked as a charlatan and celebrated as a messiah. Unyielding in his approach, Coleman committed what some considered the ultimate sin at the end of 1960 by augmenting his band to an eight-piece 'double quartet' and recording the totally improvised album-length performance *Free Jazz*.

Sounds from Saturn

Several of the ideas that Mingus, Taylor and Coleman were investigating, and others including the use of dense percussion and electric keyboards, were also surfacing in a Chicago band that had the appearance of an eccentric cult. Its leader was pianist Herman 'Sonny' Blount, a Birmingham, Alabama, native who had moved to the Midwest in the late 1930s. By 1955 Blount had renamed himself Sun Ra and formed his Arkestra, which began recording primarily on his own Saturn label in the following year. Sun Ra mixed relatively conventional hard bop concepts with more experimental ideas. He also introduced stage-show elements into his performances by dressing Arkestra members in space suits and employing vocal chants and other theatrical effects. His mystical iconoclasm would not be confined to Chicago for long.

Sun Ra, eccentric or prophet?

did you know?

Sun Ra claimed to be a messenger from outer space.

Miles and other visionaries

If one figure symbolized the ongoing evolution of jazz in 1960, it was trumpeter Miles Davis. Davis's fellow band members included innovators John Coltrane and Bill Evans.

must know

Davis's *Kind of Blue* was a watershed jazz album that continues to sell with extraordinary consistency.

After a decade of important recorded work, Miles Davis became an influential bandleader when he formed his 1955 quintet.

Miles Davis had already played bebop in Charlie Parker's band, conceived the cool jazz template with his Nonet, perfected hard bop on his early albums and with his stunning working Quintet, and expanded orchestral possibilities in his conceptually rich projects with Gil Evans. In 1959 Davis took an idea that had long fascinated him – playing on a sustained scale or 'mode' where harmonic 'changes' had previously been the norm – and used it as the basis for an entire album. The resulting *Kind of Blue* featured the intimacy and finely calibrated contrast of earlier Davis recordings, and added an atmosphere of mystery that in the hands of his exceptionally talented band proved more seductive than threatening.

The Davis band at the time was a sextet with the imposing personnel of saxophonists Cannonball Adderley and John Coltrane, pianists Bill Evans or Wynton Kelly (both appear on the album), bassist Paul Chambers and drummer Jimmy Cobb. It had not performed the new modal compositions (many of which had been developed by Evans from a series of chord symbols provided by Davis) on a regular basis, yet it responded to the new forms with exceptional eloquence in the recording studio. In the short term, *Kind of Blue* provided critical inspiration to the trumpeter's two most brilliant sidemen.

Out from under the sheets

John Coltrane was already a leading hard bopper by 1959, having perfected a knowledge of harmony and a ferocious attack that produced rapid arpeggios, memorably dubbed 'sheets of sound' by critic Ira Gitler. Modal jazz presented new melodic and rhythmic possibilities that complemented Coltrane's growing fascination with the extended interplay of lead voice and percussion in the music of Indian sitar master Ravi Shankar.

Coltrane quickly applied these concepts in the quartet he formed in 1960, with critical assists from the hypnotic piano patterns of McCoy Tyner and the dense polyrhythms of drummer Elvin Jones. Coltrane also began to alternate between tenor and soprano saxophones, bringing the latter instrument (still primarily identified with Sidney Bechet and New Orleans traditionalists) firmly into the contemporary realm. The soprano's nasal, 'Eastern' sound was featured on Coltrane's popular 1960 interpretation of the Broadway show tune 'My Favorite Things'.

Apprenticeships with both Davis and Thelonious Monk prepared John Coltrane to enter the 1960s as a bandleader.

Bill Evans also prepared for leading his innovative piano trio with a stint in the Davis band.

Liberating the piano trio

Bill Evans took modal options in a more introverted yet equally impressive direction. When Evans left Davis to form his own trio in 1959, he sought to redefine both song structures and the functions of piano, bass and drums. Previous trio music, as exemplified by Bud Powell, Erroll Garner and Oscar Peterson, relegated the bass and drums primarily to time-keeping roles. Even the schemes of Ahmad Jamal assumed limited flexibility for the supporting instruments. Evans's new trio was more of a collective enterprise where the lead might shift among the players several times within the length of a single chorus. Bassist Scott LaFaro added virtuosic countermelodies rather than strict walking lines, and drummer Paul Motian moved around rather than on the beat. The harmonically advanced Evans, who had helped turn Davis's modal ideas into compositions for *Kind of Blue*, continued to perfect his complex voicings in the trio context, creating impressionistic colours with a brittle edge that would soon become common coin for several generations of jazz pianists.

Looking ahead

Davis's band had been diminished by 1960, as Evans, Adderley and finally Coltrane left to organize their own groups. Still, the trumpeter's list of achievements, already as rich and diverse as anyone's save Duke Ellington's, promised further innovations to come. In little more than a decade, Miles Davis had made the case that jazz was a miraculous engine of change and suggested that those changes had not run their course.

want to know more?

The albums listed below, along with the musicians or groups who performed them, are some of the highlights of the era.

- **Cannonball Adderley**
  Quintet Live in San Francisco
- **Louis Armstrong**
  Satchmo at Symphony Hall
- **Count Basie**
  E=mc²
- **Sidney Bechet**
  Up a Lazy River
- **Art Blakey**
  Moanin'
- **Clifford Brown/Max Roach**
  Brown/Roach, Inc. at Basin Street
- **Dave Brubeck**
  Jazz Goes to College
- *Ray Charles at Newport*
- **Nat 'King' Cole**
  The Very Best of Nat King Cole
- **Ornette Coleman**
  The Shape of Jazz to Come
- **John Coltrane**
  Giant Steps
- **Tadd Dameron/Fats Navarro**
  The Fabulous Fats Navarro, Vol. 1
- **Miles Davis**
  Birth of the Cool
  Kind of Blue
  Relaxin' with the Miles Davis Quintet
- **Miles Davis/Gil Evans**
  Sketches of Spain
- **Duke Ellington**
  Never No Lament: The Webster/Blanton Band
  Ellington at Newport 1956
- **Bill Evans**
  Portrait in Jazz
- **Ella Fitzgerald Sings the George and Ira Gershwin Song Book**
- **Dizzy Gillespie**
  The Complete RCA Victor Recordings

- **Gillespie/Parker/Powell/ Mingus/Roach**
  Jazz at Massey Hall
- **Lionel Hampton**
  Hamp: The Legendary Decca Recordings
- **Woody Herman**
  Thundering Herds 1945–1947
- **Louis Jordan**
  The Best of Louis Jordan
- **Stan Kenton**
  City of Glass
- **Machito**
  Afro-Cuban Jazz Suite
- **Charles Mingus**
  Mingus Ah Um
- **Modern Jazz Quartet**
  Fontessa
- **Thelonious Monk**
  Genius of Modern Music, Vols 1 & 2
  Brilliant Corners
- **Gerry Mulligan**
  The Original Quartet with Chet Baker
- **Charlie Parker**
  The Complete Savoy and Dial Master Takes
- **Oscar Peterson**
  The Jazz Soul of Oscar Peterson
- **Bud Powell**
  The Amazing Bud Powell, Vols 1 & 2
- **Shorty Rogers**
  Modern Sounds
- **Sonny Rollins**
  Saxophone Colossus
- **Horace Silver and the Jazz Messengers**
- **Frank Sinatra**
  In the Wee Small Hours
- **Sun Ra**
  Jazz in Silhouette
- **Lennie Tristano**
  Intuition

4 Freedom and fusion (1961–1980)

The spirit of discovery continued to thrive as jazz entered the 1960s, a decade known for radical rethinking in other realms of art and in the political sphere. New styles took jazz in different directions, adjusting the already-expanded term in diverse ways that renewed debates about what sounds did and did not merit the name 'jazz'.

Shock of the new

Two widely shared goals – to gain greater freedom in the jazz process by abandoning or revising traditional rules of form and technique, and to merge the elements that made jazz special with other idioms – led some of the period's music to be designated under such names as free jazz and fusion.

Blood Sweat and Tears was among the first rock bands to explicitly reflect the influence of jazz.

Sun Ra and Arkestra were among the first to take the music in the direction of unfettered freedom.

The line between such styles and more traditional approaches, or between one such style and another, was often unclear. Still, the new directions that jazz pursued in the 1960s made it more difficult to find common threads among the new styles – a difficulty that had existed since at least the decline of big bands. In the case of free jazz, or avant-garde jazz or simply 'the New Thing' as it was called in its early years, the embrace of jazz as a high art, disposed by its irreverence and improvised cohesion to deal in greater abstraction, went far beyond many listeners who looked to music primarily for entertainment.

These explorations of new sounds, rhythmic systems and shapes for improvised performances did little to persuade the many classical music and

cultural commentators who continued to find jazz's roots and its celebrated heroes on the other side of the art/entertainment divide. But by the end of the 1970s, the free players (now as likely to settle for the designation 'creative improvisers') had taken their ideas both into the American interior and around the world, demanding an acceptance on their own terms that many would receive in later decades.

Jazz in a rock world

What first appeared as jazz-rock or electric jazz in the late 1960s, and gained the one-word title 'fusion' by the middle of the following decade, grew in part out of the notion that jazz did retain a connection to popular taste, especially as that taste evolved in an era defined by new ideas in pop music. This meant transforming the nature of the ensemble sound through amplification, greater reliance on electric and electronically enhanced instruments, and beats that grew out of rock and roll, and soul music as well as swing.

American pop music had followed the example set by early jazz styles in becoming the common language of international youth culture, which gave fusion's innovators a more international profile than other jazz generations, even as the greater availability of other ethnic musics suggested additional cross-cultural hybrids. Yet not all such syntheses were electric, and not all fusion escaped the more mechanical and tepid strategies of the era's lesser pop music. As rock-inflected jazz placed greater emphasis on glossy production and less on improvisational surprise, the term 'fusion' became a pejorative to many, a six-letter dismissal of music that lacked daring and a willingness to test more spontaneous, uncharted concepts.

The mixture of thematic simplicity and sonic extremity in Albert Ayler's music remains among the jazz world's most controversial sounds.

A generation of generations

While these new ideas were encountering various degrees of acceptance and resistance, jazz as it had already come to be known continued to be practised by diverse musicians of diverse ages and styles.

> **must know**
>
> From its most traditional forms to more progressive recent approaches, and points in between, every aspect of the music we call 'jazz' could be heard in the 1960s and 1970s.

Many veterans sustained their creativity or hit new peaks, while a new cohort of aspiring musicians found growing opportunities to learn the finer points of earlier styles in high school and college music programmes. The survival and in some cases ongoing brilliance of several living legends alongside younger and more radical stylists reinforced the breadth of the period's jazz, as illustrated by the ever-widening juxtapositions found in the programmes of the growing number of jazz festivals. When these same giants died, their passing invariably called into question ultimate judgments regarding the music's ongoing health.

John Coltrane, bandleader

The quartet that John Coltrane formed in 1960, featuring McCoy Tyner's piano and Elvin Jones's drums almost from the outset, and completed in its classic form when Jimmy Garrison became the permanent bassist two years later, provided a surprisingly popular focal point for freer expression through the first years of the decade. The intense power and focus of the quartet, its ability to incorporate African and Indian influences through its use of modes and scales, and the added contrast available now that Coltrane played both tenor and soprano saxophones marked this as one of the great groups in jazz history.

While nightclub and festival recordings gave some indication of the impassioned extended improvisations that the band created in person (many of which exceeded the bounds of the 20-minute LP side), the quartet's music retained enough rhythmic definition and blues' motifs to make its connection to earlier jazz styles irrefutable. Coltrane underscored these links with studio projects that included an eloquent programme of ballads and partnerships with vocalist Johnny Hartman and Duke Ellington. Ellington's collaboration with Coltrane confirmed that many of the latter's ideas could coexist with the concepts of jazz royalty.

The early 1960s can be viewed as Duke Ellington's 'collaborative' period, as he partnered with a spectrum of jazz giants.

Host with the most

Between 1961 and 1962, Ellington was heard in the piano chair of Louis Armstrong's All Stars, leading his orchestra as half of a two-band summit with Count Basie's troops, in an octet encounter with tenor sax patriarch Coleman Hawkins, a quartet with Coltrane, and a rambunctious trio completed by Charles Mingus and Max Roach. While continuing to write new music, including symphonic settings of several extended works and the theatrical presentation *My People*, at least for the first years of the 1960s Ellington's most memorable creations were found in his collaborative work. At least for this musician, and at least for the present, it was clear that jazz could be more about personal connection than about stylistic division.

did you know?

The Ellington-Coltrane collaboration is one of several historical pairings that bolstered Ellington's image as jazz's most inclusive genius.

OPPOSITE: **Among his many important contributions, John Coltrane brought the soprano saxophone back to the centre of jazz creativity.**

Connecting to outside influences

During this period, jazz musicians encountered several external influences, including bossa nova and Third Stream. These new styles were met with varying degrees of enthusiasm.

A new wrinkle from South America

One of the Ellington band's more popular albums of the period, *Afro Bossa*, alludes in its title to a musical style from Brazil known as bossa nova ('a new wrinkle', in Brazilian slang). It featured a modification of traditional samba rhythm and a lyrical, harmonically sophisticated body of compositions that were tailor-made for jazz soloists. Composer/pianist Antonio Carlos Jobim and singer/guitarist João Gilberto began composing in the style in 1958. Its rapid success did not go unnoticed by jazz musicians such as Dizzy Gillespie, Herbie Mann and Charlie Byrd, who heard the bossa nova during tours of South America and were among the first to record Jobim's songs in jazz settings.

Byrd and Stan Getz, whose tender sound and melodic resources were ideal for bossa nova, turned the hybrid style into an instant trend with their 1962 album *Jazz Samba*, which featured the hit single 'Desafinado'. The album's success was exceeded when Getz, Gilberto and the singer's wife Astrud were teamed a year later in an album highlighted by Jobim's 'Girl from Ipanema'. Other jazz found a place on the best-seller charts during the early 1960s, including the Dave Brubeck Quartet's 'Take Five', Jimmy Smith's 'Walk on the Wild Side' and Ramsey Lewis's 'The In Crowd', but for those with an eye to record sales it was Getz's sambas that defined 'popular' jazz in the period.

Stan Getz's tenor sax was the perfect vehicle for popularizing the bossa nova sounds of composer Antonio Carlos Jobim (seen here playing guitar).

A stream apart

Another attempt to connect jazz with outside influences, Third Stream, proved more controversial and less popular. Championed most vocally by John Lewis of the Modern Jazz Quartet and composer Gunther Schuller, Third Stream was a conscious effort to create a new and distinct synthesis from the existing tributaries of jazz and classical music. Some performances that embraced the label, including the Schuller compositions in the album *Jazz Abstractions*, and others that did not but might well have (specifically *Focus*, which featured Stan Getz improvising over Eddie Sauter's string settings), succeeded in pairing improvisers with chamber musicians. But the lack of performance opportunities and the relative scarcity of musicians who could function convincingly in both realms doomed most Third Stream attempts to little more than curiosity status.

Jazz works with classical ambition pre-dated Third Stream and would continue to be created in its wake, but the concept itself generated little momentum. By the time Schuller, as president of the New England Conservatory, introduced a Third Stream curriculum in the 1970s, the term had taken on the broader meaning of any disparate musics merged into a personal idiom.

must know

Antonio Carlos Jobim's body of work put him in a league with the likes of songwriters Gershwin and Porter – and the sounds and rhythms of Brazilian percussion instruments became standards in many contemporary jazz performances.

Composer Gunther Schuller hoped to merge jazz and classical music into a 'Third Stream'.

The expanding mainstream

While some looked for new directions, a myriad of established jazz styles displayed continued health, revealing the breadth of artists and music that jazz had come to embrace.

Pee Wee Russell's last years proved that great jazz was still being made by those who pre-dated the modern era.

Coleman Hawkins and Pee Wee Russell entered their senior years with impressive small-group recordings. Count Basie sustained his big band through pairings with Ella Fitzgerald and Frank Sinatra, while both Woody Herman and Stan Kenton found renewed relevance with reorganized orchestras. Dave Brubeck and the Modern Jazz Quartet remained popular in concert settings, while Dizzy Gillespie joined his former saxophonist James Moody and young pianist Kenny Barron in one of his best quintets.

Hard bop, often with added emphasis on soulful blues and gospel inflections, enjoyed a growing audience thanks to the bands of Cannonball Adderley, Art Blakey and Horace Silver, while Miles Davis took his first steps into more abstract territory with a new quintet powered by the elasticity of a rhythm section featuring pianist Herbie Hancock, bassist Ron Carter and drummer Tony Williams. Oscar Peterson and Ahmad Jamal continued to define the more extroverted and controlled concepts of the piano trio, respectively.

Redefining virtuosity

Two new stars took radical approaches to their instruments. Guitarist John 'Wes' Montgomery used his thumb rather than a pick to extract a warm, personal sound from his instrument, then built his

must know

Wes Montgomery defined new standards for jazz guitar and became the instrument's dominant influence.

Two of the most innovative instrumentalists of the early 1960s were guitarist Wes Montgomery (*far left*) and multi-instrumentalist Rahsaan Roland Kirk (*left*).

solos from lucid single lines to more dazzling choruses filled with intervals and chords. While comfortable in a range of settings and committed to straight-ahead jazz in his public performances, Montgomery produced increasingly conservative readings of pop songs on recordings as the decade progressed. When a heart attack ended his life in 1968, he had become a pop phenomenon with little jazz content on his albums.

While Ronald 'Roland' Kirk never achieved Montgomery's commercial success, or anything approaching a similar legion of imitators, his ability to play three saxophones at once, harmonize with guttural vocals while improvising on flute and punctuate solos with sirens and whistles was equally innovative. The blind Kirk's trademark sunglasses, odd array of instruments and rough-edged demeanour gave him the appearance of a jazz shaman. Kirk was consumed by music, in all forms and styles. Prior to his death in 1978, he had even found a way to continue performing after a stroke had left one side of his body paralysed.

did you know?

At the end of the 1960s, Ronald 'Roland' Kirk adopted the name Rahsaan and rechristened his group The Vibration Society.

Accolades for Hines and Monk

The career boosts that two of jazz's greatest pianists
received during 1964 illustrate the richness of the
music in this period. Earl Hines, who had been living in
San Francisco virtually unnoticed for more than a
decade, performed a series of solo and quartet
concerts in New York that led to his rediscovery.
Numerous recordings and appearances, including a
tour of the Soviet Union in 1966, revived Hines's status
as an innovator who could still deliver technically
dazzling and emotionally rich performances, a position
he sustained with several poll victories and a slew of
solo piano collections that carried him through the
1970s.

Thelonious Monk, a more iconoclastic presence,
gained even more widespread recognition when the
growing acceptance of his music and regular visits to
Europe and Japan by his working quartet landed him
on the cover of *Time* magazine. Monk retained the
small-group format until he retired from performing at
the start of the next decade.

A piano trio paragon

Another pianist who stayed true to his preferences
was Bill Evans, whose unique voicings, touch and
sense of ensemble interactivity revealed new
possibilities for the piano trio. There were departures
from the format in the ensuing 20 years, including
the astonishing multitracked 1963 recording
Conversations with Myself, but even the death of
bassist Scott LaFaro in a 1961 road accident did not
inspire Evans to abandon the trio setting. Until his
own death in 1980, Evans continued to work in the
company of technically dazzling bassists who

sustained intense colloquies with his keyboard and drummers who were as likely to imply as to state the beat. He created a body of work in the process that had an enormous influence on the pianists who followed.

A music of wide horizons

Two seminal recordings from the middle of the decade illustrate the breadth of jazz at this time. At the end of 1963, Louis Armstrong's All Stars gave a traditional New Orleans reading to the theme song from the new Broadway musical *Hello, Dolly*. Released as a single several months later, Armstrong's 'Hello, Dolly' proved so popular that, even at the height of Beatlemania, it briefly became the best-selling single of the day. Almost exactly one year later, John Coltrane's quartet taped its masterpiece *A Love Supreme*, a four-part suite expressing Coltrane's growing spirituality that captured this immortal ensemble at its peak and was showered with accolades.

OPPOSITE: **Decades after their initial innovations, pianists Earl Hines (*top*) and Thelonious Monk (*bottom*) gained new stature during the 1960s.**

LEFT: **While Bill Evans experimented with multitracked solo recording, he continued to work in the trio context.**

Freedom's forefathers

Amid all of this diverse musical activity, the quest for a freer form of jazz expression gained momentum at the start of the 1960s. The refinements of modern jazz giants Mingus and Coltrane reinforced the discoveries of Ornette Coleman and Cecil Taylor, who began at the borders of jazz orthodoxy and continued to push further afield.

did you know?

In the mid-1960s a group of young New York firebrands formed the Jazz Composers Guild, mounted a concert series billed as a 'revolution' and demanded that the new music be acknowledged.

Charles Mingus's open forms were taking on bolder shapes and denser colours in such compositions as 'The Black Saint and the Sinner Lady' and 'Meditations on Integration'. Coleman, who had abandoned chorus structure and recurring chord patterns in his early quartet work, had expanded these concepts into other realms by 1962, when a concert of his music at Town Hall in New York included works for string quartet and rhythm and blues band. Taylor's preference for kinetic energy and harmonic density had taken him into more unfettered areas even earlier, as the music he recorded beginning in 1961 set aside such conventions as a sustained beat and allowed his piano accompaniments to confront and often overwhelm the soloists in his ensembles.

Sun Ra, the intergalactic innovator who moved his entire Arkestra from Chicago to New York in 1961, showed how these various forms of licence could be applied in larger ensembles. Established players were moved to adjust their styles as well. Clarinetist Jimmy Giuffre's gentle folk jazz turned more spare and impulsive once Canadian pianist Paul Bley joined his trio. Tenor saxophonist Sonny Rollins began working with former Ornette Coleman associates in 1962. And alto saxophonist Jackie McLean proclaimed that the New Thing had liberated his thinking in

adventurous albums such as *Let Freedom Ring*, which alternated with projects in his more familiar hard bop style.

Coltrane's free finale

John Coltrane was an obvious candidate for godfather to the free players. He perpetually tested limits with his own music, eagerly placed added stress on spiritual concerns, and served as the sole example of a jazz experimenter who sustained a large public following. He fulfilled his godfather role admirably, by including several of the new stylists in his controversial 1965 recordings *Ascension* and *Meditations*, and by persuading his record label Impulse! to offer contracts to younger free players, including saxophonists Albert Ayler, Marion Brown, Farrell 'Pharoah' Sanders and Archie Shepp.

Ties that Coltrane had sustained with more conventional modernists, especially the rugged swing of his classic rhythm section, became frayed when his wife Alice Coltrane replaced McCoy Tyner and drummer Elvin Jones ceded his chair to Rashied Ali. Coltrane's own failing health led him to lean more heavily on the exhortations of Sanders in live performances. Coltrane's style, never given to a sense that it had settled, promised a new period of sweeping lyricism in his final studio recordings from early 1967,

did you know?

The early 1970s saw New York's freedom movement driven further underground and further away from the centres of jazz performance, into the warehouses and lofts of the Lower East Side.

but liver cancer claimed his life that July, three months short of his 41st birthday.

At a loss for a leader

John Coltrane's death, the focus for many practitioners for aligning their music with political liberation and spiritual/mystical movements, and the growing public interest in the new electric forms of jazz discussed below are all frequently noted as reasons why so many of the free jazz were unable to attract a larger audience. Ornette Coleman and Cecil Taylor may have gained some acceptance as innovators (a view confirmed by their brief affiliation with the already legendary Blue Note label at the end of the 1960s), but opportunities to hear either of them in person or on record remained rare well into the next decade and beyond. Albert Ayler blended simple melodies, extreme saxophone techniques and combustible ensemble interaction that made him the most unique and compelling of the second innovative wave. He might have functioned as the new music's focal point, but a turn towards simplistic rhythm and blues in 1968 and his mysterious death two years later ended that prospect.

The death of Albert Ayler in 1970 ended one of the oddest stylistic journeys of the period.

Think free, play locally

Even before Coltrane's death, young African American musicians had decided that a better way to cultivate new music might involve the nurturing of new ideas in more supportive local communities. Others left the country to explore the broader horizons of Europe.

As a complement to the political activism that endorsed Black Power, young black musicians began incorporating organizations that would focus on the ideas of Coltrane, Coleman, Taylor and Ayler in conjunction with a more Afro-centric and interdisciplinary approach to music that viewed jazz as a primary but hardly exclusive expression of the African Diaspora. Los Angeles pianist Horace Tapscott organized one such early group, the Pan-Afrikan Peoples Arkestra in 1961.

While many of the resulting works presented under the general structure of these organizations included theatre, poetry and dance, the musical

must know

The founding of the Association for the Advancement of Creative Music in 1965 spawned a collection of similar groups, including the Creative Artists Collective in Detroit and the Black Artists Group in St Louis.

Muhal Richard Abrams did not have to go to New York to make his innovations felt throughout the jazz world.

Roscoe Mitchell was the first of Chicago's AACM to record as a bandleader, and he remains among its most audacious creators.

innovations of the Association for the Advancement of Creative Music (AACM) could be heard in the early recordings of pianist and founder Muhal Richard Abrams and saxophonists Roscoe Mitchell and Anthony Braxton. Their compositional structures abandoned strict theme and variation strategies. They used 'found objects' and other 'little instruments' for new percussive colours and juxtaposed diverse and unlikely instrumental groupings. A new focus on unaccompanied performance for all instrumentalists rounded out these local innovations.

Spreading freedom overseas

By 1969 it had become clear that even hometown loyalties could not create an American audience large enough to sustain the experimenters, and several AACM members departed for Europe in bands that became known as the Art Ensemble of Chicago (Mitchell, trumpeter Lester Bowie, saxophonist Joseph Jarman, bassist Malachi Favors) and the Creative Construction Company (Braxton, trumpeter Leo Smith, violinist Leroy Jenkins, drummer Steve McCall). They sought a more serious acceptance of their music and a less segregated lifestyle, as other more established jazz artists (including saxophonist Dexter Gordon, Johnny Griffin and Steve Lacy, trumpeter Don Cherry and composer/theorist George Russell) had earlier in the decade. They did encounter more receptive audiences, who had learned to take jazz seriously as art in advance of most listeners in America, and they also found local musicians eager to create a personal voice of their own under the ever-widening jazz umbrella.

German saxophonist Peter Brötzmann, Dutch pianist Misha Mengelberg, British saxophonist Evan Parker and guitarist Derek Bailey, and Italian trumpeter Enrico Rava were among those who brought their own experimental proclivities to the conversation. After most of the American free players had returned to the United States, it was these Europeans who remained and created a different kind of localized avant-garde.

Innovation with a rock accent

At the same moment that Coltrane's embrace of the new music had sparked controversy, another group of musicians were starting to wonder if jazz's future might lie in a rapprochement with evolving pop music styles. The Beatles had demonstrated that rock could possess substance and ambition, while other rock bands such as Cream and The Grateful Dead were making extended improvisation part of their performances. The enormous

By 1970 a great deal of the free jazz scene had shifted to Europe, thanks to both the expatriation of such artists as Steve Lacy (*left*) and the rise of homegrown explorers like England's Evan Parker (*right*).

Charles Lloyd was among the first to bring a rock performance sensibility to jazz.

popularity of these groups had its own appeal to many jazz musicians who, even when acknowledged as masters within the jazz world, remained on the fringes of commercial success. But many younger players who grew up enjoying rock and roll, and who identified with the cultural aspects of the new pop music, found an affinity of their own.

The connection was clear in the music of saxophonist/flutist Charles Lloyd, whose quartet recorded its often psychedelic-tinged music at San Francisco's Fillmore Auditorium in 1967, and even more audible when vibraphonist Gary Burton formed a quartet featuring Larry Coryell's rock-saturated guitar that same year. Tenor saxophonist Eddie Harris began playing his horn through electronic attachments and gave instrumental jazz a funkier sound with his hit 'Listen Here'.

must know

A jazz-rock era had dawned, and the fusion deluge would follow – after receiving the blessing of one of the jazz world's reigning stars, Miles Davis.

Both Gary Burton's wardrobe and his use of the electric guitar made his 1967 quartet one of the first harbingers of jazz-rock.

Switched-on Miles

The mantle of innovator that Miles Davis had worn through so much of his earlier career had been regained by 1965, when saxophonist/composer Wayne Shorter joined the trumpeter, Herbie Hancock, Ron Carter and Tony Williams in what became known as the second classic Miles Davis quintet.

That band's ability to take hard bop and modal ideas to the very edge of free-form, and the prolific bent of Davis's sidemen plus Coltrane alumni McCoy Tyner and Elvin Jones on numerous studio recordings, were already giving a more contemporary 'postbop' cast to modernism. Even so, this was not enough for Davis, who grew fascinated by the music of James Brown, Jimi Hendrix and Sly Stone as the decade progressed. The example of these pop innovators, plus a growing fondness for the sonic potential of amplified instruments, inspired the trumpeter to employ electric keyboards and electric bass in his quintet, as first heard on his 1968 album *Filles de Kilimanjaro*. He added multiple keyboards, electric guitar, miscellaneous percussion, processed sound and abrupt splicing on subsequent recordings. While the term 'fusion' had yet to be applied, the era of what was still called jazz-rock had arrived in no uncertain terms.

> **must know**
>
> Miles Davis's 1969 *Bitches Brew* album displayed all the new 'jazz-rock' features in what became one of Davis's most popular recordings.

Sons of *Bitches*

For an index of the most important and successful musicians in the new electric style, one hardly need look beyond the ranks of Davis's working and recording bands of the period. Herbie Hancock, already leading his own sextet by 1968, quickly added electric keyboards, synthesizer and other effects, only to abandon the

did you know?

Herbie Hancock's
sextet became
known as his
Mwandishi band, a
reference to
Hancock's Swahili
name.

resultant psychedelic aura in favour of a tighter, funkier emphasis in his still-electric Headhunters group of 1973.

Armando 'Chick' Corea, Hancock's replacement with Davis, went through a few iterations of his own, beginning with the avant-garde quartet Circle that also included AACM stalwart Anthony Braxton. Corea's first edition of Return to Forever placed electric keyboards and bass in a samba context. He then quickly reworked RTF as a heavily amplified power quartet with electric guitar.

Drummer Tony Williams came closest to the high-decibel onslaught of the Jimi Hendrix Experience with Lifetime, a trio including organist Larry Young and *Bitches Brew* guitarist John McLaughlin. Williams's band never enjoyed the popular success of the Mahavishnu Orchestra, the quintet McLaughlin founded in 1971 that added an emphasis on odd meters and virtuosic ensemble execution to Lifetime's dynamic bombast. Original Mahavishnu drummer and occasional Miles Davis session man Billy Cobham then founded his own band, which helped establish the likes of trumpeter Randy Brecker and

Herbie Hancock's
incorporation of electric
keyboards gave another
indication that some of
the jazz world's leading
figures were ready to
move in a rock direction.

Tony Williams would
lose the jacket and tie
once he formed his
seminal Lifetime trio.

his younger brother, saxophonist Michael, and guitarists John Abercrombie and John Scofield.

Changes of weather

Wayne Shorter, whose writing had contributed so much to Miles Davis's recent evolution, and Josef Zawinul, whose use of an electric piano in the Cannonball Adderley band had first caught Davis's attention, found a steadier source of inspiration in Weather Report, the cooperative band that they organized in 1970. Heavily electric yet close to free music in its earliest incarnation, Weather Report began to place greater emphasis on sustained grooves in 1973. It continued to refine its music with a tighter compositional focus, diverse melodic and rhythmic flavourings from other cultures, and a sonic range that expanded as Zawinul added newly invented keyboards and effects.

While Zawinul and Shorter were constants, diverse players passed through Weather Report's rhythm section, none more talented or charismatic than John 'Jaco' Pastorius, whose virtuosic electric bass and compositions helped define his 1976–1982 tenure as the band's golden era.

Weather Report *circa* 1975: (*left to right*) Chester Thompson, Wayne Shorter, Joe Zawinul, Alyrio Lima and Alphonso Johnson.

Voices in treacherous times

As free jazz and fusion became focal points of the era, many established musicians found opportunities to work and record growing scarce. Though vocalists identified with jazz and popular standards found the situation perilous, some big bands came up with ways to adapt.

Established stars such as Tony Bennett, Ella Fitzgerald, Carmen McRae, Sarah Vaughan, Joe Williams and even Frank Sinatra had to gear their output to the youth market or go for long stretches without issuing new albums. This situation prevailed throughout the 1970s, although Fitzgerald and Vaughan ultimately found an outlet when Norman Granz reemerged in the record business with the Pablo label in 1973.

Artist-owned record companies were another option, though one that would take time to catch on. Two singers who pioneered in such do-it-yourself efforts were Bennett, who released one of two spellbinding duet sessions with pianist Bill Evans on his own Improv label, and the still unknown Betty Carter, whose frustration with the treatment afforded by established companies led her to issue some of the 1970s' most inspired vocal jazz under her own Bet-Car imprint.

Betty Carter was both an influential vocalist and a pioneer in artist-owned recording companies.

Big bands in transition

Some leaders of the jazz big bands who drew heavily on the graduates of music schools for their players (Maynard Ferguson, Woody Herman and the ensemble Buddy Rich assembled in 1966) found themselves absorbing a younger complement of accompanists willing to play contemporary pop and rock material alongside more 'straight ahead' jazz. Others who were more concerned with employing a band's forces in personal expression had greater difficulty facing the economic challenges of sustaining a large group.

A new prototype was developed by trumpeter Thad Jones, who formed a band with drummer Mel Lewis in order to rehearse his own original material and then found a Monday night home for the Jones/Lewis Jazz Orchestra at New York's Village Vanguard. Soon such respected writers as Gerald Wilson, Bill Holman, Toshiko Akiyoshi and Gil Evans established themselves at the head of such regular/irregular units.

Snubbing, and celebrating, the Duke

One big band that persevered was the Duke Ellington Orchestra, which had produced a half-century of quality music by the time of its leader's death in 1974. In 1965 the Pulitzer Prize committee rejected a special award in Ellington's honour. After jesting that Fate considered him too young to receive such accolades, Ellington – whose body of work had reached Pulitzer status at least 30 years earlier – provided a response in his final decade that included three Concerts of Sacred Music, several suite-length reflections on his world travels and hundreds of new shorter songs, all while keeping his band working constantly.

Some of the music was created during tours sponsored by the U.S. government, and the White House (which he first visited during Harry Truman's administration) saw fit to host Ellington's 70th birthday celebration in 1969. This act of public acceptance signalled a growing appreciation of jazz, if not the level of public and private non-profit support due to those seeking to follow in Ellington's footsteps.

> **did you know?**
> 'Kicks' bands of the 1960s were formed by musicians looking for personal satisfaction rather than economic sustenance.

While work was scarce, bandleaders such as Toshiko Akiyoshi found ways to realize their orchestral ambitions.

Playing surfaces

Where music gets played can often influence how music sounds, and there is no denying that location accelerated various musical changes in the period.

Concert halls and nightclubs remained the worksites of most jazz musicians. The growth of arena and stadium presentations in the pop realm proved more accommodating to highly amplified fusion bands, while the lofts, galleries and studio spaces that became home for the free players led some of the most daring to explore both the quiet as well as the explosive ends of the dynamic spectrum.

All jazz styles were more likely to be heard at the growing number of festivals that became an international phenomenon. Destination events included those held in Montreux, Switzerland (established 1967), New Orleans (1969) and the worldwide skein generated by Newport founder George Wein's Festival Productions. As pop music became more serious and pressures to ensure a profit grew more intense, the jazz content at

Festivals such as the one held in Montreux, Switzerland, provided the arena-like settings that suited jazz in its fusion incarnation.

some jazz festivals diminished. Occasionally this brought conflict, as in Newport; elsewhere, as in Montreux, jazz was simply dropped from the festival title. Yet festivals that did focus on jazz also proliferated, placing focus on everything from the early New Orleans tradition to the most extreme creative edge.

New looks, new labels

The spread of jazz festivals to such locales as Molde in Norway, Perugia in Italy and Osaka in Japan mirrored the development of jazz recording into a truly international industry. New labels continued to emerge in the United States, but the declining interest of the established major labels, and the decline of former independents as they were acquired by larger companies with other priorities, led many musicians in a variety of styles to look beyond American borders for recording opportunities. By the end of the 1970s a list of the most active jazz labels would include not only the new U.S. imprints Concord, Muse and Pablo, but also Denmark's SteepleChase, Italy's Black Saint/Soul Note and the Dutch label Timeless.

U.S. labels re-issued a wealth of classic music. The deluxe boxed-set collections of the 1960s gave way to double-jacketed 'twofers' in the 1970s. Even more could be found in facsimile packaging designed for the Japanese market. Two new labels, one based in New York, the other in Cologne, Germany, and each with a three-letter name, showed a knack for defining contemporary musical styles.

Monogramming popular jazz

In the case of the American CTI, the initials connoted the corporate enterprise of Creed Taylor, a veteran record producer who had refined an audience-friendly approach in his work with Stan Getz, Wes Montgomery and others

Producer Creed Taylor had a knack for aural and visual packaging of jazz that helped expand its audience base.

The early 1970s found some musicians, including the Crusaders (*above*), adding rock and funk elements to what had been their jazz profile, while others such as Grover Washington, Jr (*below*) emerged as new stars in the hybrid idiom.

before launching his own imprint in 1970. CTI albums tended to feature acknowledged jazz soloists (including guitarist George Benson, trumpeter Freddie Hubbard, vibist Milt Jackson and tenor saxophonist Stanley Turrentine) surrounded by tight, pop-oriented rhythm sections and the occasional sweetening of overdubbed horns and strings. All were given a vibrant sonic gloss by engineer Rudy Van Gelder. The pop-art sizzle of fold-out covers featured the fashionable photography of Pete Turner.

To an even greater extent than earlier labels, the look of a CTI album became synonymous with its sound, best exemplified by saxophonist Grover Washington, Jr, who only recorded the first of his many hit albums for CTI subsidiary Kudu when the scheduled bandleader failed to appear. Well before his most popular album *Winelight* was released in 1980, Washington, with the help of streamlined orchestrations and the occasional guest vocalist, had turned his contemporary mix of jazz and rhythm and blues into a pop phenomenon.

George Benson enjoyed even greater success as his vocals eclipsed his initial fame as a guitarist, and pianist/arranger Bob James (one of Washington's early collaborators) proved reliable enough as both producer and solo artist to launch his own label. Jazz, or more specifically the jazz delivered in this subdued, soulful form, was reaching a mass audience again.

The band that laboured through the 1960s as the hard-bop-oriented Jazz Crusaders added electric guitar and electric bass, turned its focus in similarly funky directions and revealed indifference to issues of jazz authenticity by changing its name to The Crusaders and enjoying previously unprecedented success.

A more rarefied gloss

More comprehensive, international fusions also took place in the 1970s, as American artists looked beyond traditional sources to incorporate ideas from other countries, and improvisers from these diverse cultures in turn made an impression upon jazz.

The music's proliferation on record, radio and in concert had truly created a global village with room for South African pianist Abdullah Ibrahim (a.k.a. Dollar Brand), the folk-oriented quartet Oregon, John McLaughlin's raga-rooted band Shakti, Brazilian percussion wizard Airto Moreira, and a host of Europeans with their own bold personalities and personal systems.

Manfred Eicher's ECM, founded in Germany in 1969, epitomized this eclectic internationalism. Out of his training as a symphonic bassist and his love for the music of Miles Davis and Paul Bley, Eicher generated impeccably sounding chamber music, clean yet brooding, heavy with tones and recurring patterns reverberating in an ever-present (even if only sensed) background of ominous silence. The assertive rhythms of classic and modern jazz and the colorations of the blues were often at a premium in the work of ECM stalwarts such as Norwegian saxophonist Jan Garbarek and German bassist Eberhard Weber, but the kinship of much of the music heard on ECM to serious jazz was unmistakable.

did you know?
'ECM' stands for 'Editions of Contemporary Music'.

Eclectic mastery

While the austerity of both ECM's sound and its cover art led some to claim that it too was fostering stylistic

Keith Jarrett was one of the period's most prolific and popular jazz artists, gaining success as a solo pianist and leader of two distinctive quartets.

regimentation, the best and most acclaimed artists on its roster thrived on diversity, none more so than the multi-talented Keith Jarrett. A pianist who saw the dawn of the jazz/rock merger in Charles Lloyd's original quartet, and who briefly assumed the keyboard chair in Miles Davis's band, Jarrett had rejected electric instruments and artistic compromise by the time he joined ECM in 1971. With his own boundless imagination and Eicher's unwavering support, Jarrett spent the rest of the decade composing orchestral music and sustaining both an American and a European quartet. He also performed a series of open-ended solo piano recitals that became international events and, especially on the 1975 album *The Koln Concert*, unlikely hit records.

At decade's end, Eicher found another mutable star in Pat Metheny, an American guitarist who could blur jazz, folk and pop boundaries in his working band. Metheny could also shift convincingly to postbop and free orientations in partnership with stellar saxophonists Mike Brecker and Dewey Redman, and move in the direction of impressionistic sound painting in solo projects and in his more abstract forays with pianist Lyle Mays.

Freedom's harvest

Those who pursued avant-garde paths found that even greater flexibility was required to sustain their music through the 1970s. The most ambitious and resourceful among them were represented by saxophonist/composer Anthony Braxton, whose complex, system-driven creations were heard in unaccompanied solos, duos, trios and quartets, big bands and configurations as expansive as the four simultaneously performing orchestras that recorded one of his works. Braxton displayed an affinity for European art music and rigorous compositional and rhythmic forms. An emphasis on the more visceral roots of jazz could be heard in the similarly revealing works of fellow Chicagoans Muhal Richard Abrams, Roscoe Mitchell and Henry Threadgill. Their 1970s music, as well as that of the young pianist Anthony Davis and some of the output of Ornette Coleman (whose symphony *Skies of America* was recorded in 1972), placed freedom in closer partnership with compositional structure. At the same time, Coleman's electric ensemble Prime Time and the more noise-oriented sonorities that Miles Davis favoured prior to his temporary retirement in 1975 argued that freedom and fusion could achieve another order of synthesis.

Anthony Braxton took his iconoclastic music from its AACM Chicago base to Europe before returning to the United States and achieving his greatest influence in the mid-1970s.

Alone and together

As it became harder to sustain a working group, unaccompanied solo performance assumed major importance. But the 1970s also witnessed their share of successful revivals, culminating in a White House celebration of jazz greats in 1978. The 1973 appearance of *The Smithsonian Collection of Classic Jazz* (revised 1987) was pivotal in raising public awareness of jazz as a deep and ongoing tradition.

Breaking the mould

For virtually every instrumentalist whose style could be considered post-Ornette Coleman, two solo trends developed. One involved such traditional solo instruments as piano and guitar and touched all jazz eras, while the second was the provenance of free players and also focused on saxophones, brass, bass and percussion. Many musicians (including Jarrett, Braxton, Chick Corea, guitarist Joe Pass, trombonist George Lewis and pianists Cecil Taylor, Ran Blake

The World Saxophone Quartet (left to right: Julius Hemphill, Oliver Lake, David Murray, Hamiet Bluiett) introduced a new sound, *sans* rhythm section.

and Abdullah Ibrahim) excelled in unaccompanied settings. The World Saxophone Quartet (former BAG members Hamiet Bluiett, Julius Hemphill and Oliver Lake plus young Californian David Murray) and the ROVA Saxophone Quartet, which took its name from the last initials of original members Jon Raskin, Larry Ochs, Andrew Voigt and Bruce Ackley, were each founded in the late 1970s. Both continue to expand their unique bodies of music 30 years later.

Older wines

Scott Joplin's ragtime compositions enjoyed renewed popularity after their use in the hit film *The Sting* and a series of albums by pianist Joshua Rifkin. The quartet of cornetist Ruby Braff and George Barnes, the Soprano Summit co-led by Kenny Davern and Bob Wilber, and the young tenor saxophonist Scott Hamilton brought new life to the prebop music of New Orleans, Chicago and New York. Cool innovator Lee Konitz became ubiquitous at the decade's end in a variety of groups, including a Nonet, and fellow alto saxophonist Art Pepper emerged from over a decade of drug-related incarcerations to play the most intense and warmly accepted music of his career.

Alto saxophonist Phil Woods and several other modernists returned to the United States from extended residencies in Europe, with none more heralded than Dexter Gordon, who had maintained both his facility and his commanding personality through more than a decade as an expatriate, and whose return to regular recording and performing in America became a major event in 1976. Such homecomings, together with the ongoing success of pianist McCoy Tyner, the final orchestral and small-

After years of neglect, Lee Konitz proved to be one of the more prolific and risk-taking stylists of the 1970s.

Ragtime pioneer Eubie Blake performs on the South Lawn of the White House in 1978.

must know

The 1969 White House jazz concert marked the point when many styles comprising this thing called 'jazz' had been defined.

group creations of Charles Mingus and the ability of Sonny Rollins to transcend commonplace working surroundings, gave hope for musical continuity during a decade in which Armstrong, Ellington, Mingus, Bill Evans and other innovators passed into the ranks of the immortals.

A telling celebration

On 18 June 1978, President Jimmy Carter hosted a Jazz Concert on the South Lawn of the White House to mark the 25th anniversary of the Newport Jazz Festival. The programme, which began with the rags and theatrical songs of 95-year-old pianist Eubie Blake and the blues of W. C. Handy (sung by daughter Katherine Handy Lewis), worked through small ensembles including such icons as Benny Carter, Lionel Hampton, Roy Eldridge, Illinois Jacquet, Sonny Rollins, Max Roach, Herbie Hancock and George Benson, with solo interludes from Ornette Coleman and Cecil Taylor. It was the most complete presentation of jazz in all its variations that one could imagine, and a tremendously moving experience for all in attendance, especially when President Carter embraced the wheelchair-bound Charles Mingus.

As the new decade arrived, the emphasis was poised to shift from innovation to preservation. In the heady moments of 1965, Albert Ayler had voiced the spirit of the moment when he declared, in the anthology *The New Wave in Jazz*, that 'It's not about notes any more, it's about feelings!' By the time of the White House concert, the possibility began to occur that it might no longer be about new waves either.

want to know more?

The albums listed below, along with the musicians or groups who performed them, are some of the highlights of the era.

- Louis Armstrong
  Hello, Dolly
- Air
  Air Time
  Air Lore
- Toshiko Akiyoshi/Lew Tabackin
  Long Yellow Road
- Albert Ayler
  Spiritual Unity
- Anthony Braxton
  New York Fall 1974
- Gary Burton
  Duster
- Charlie Byrd and Stan Getz
  Jazz Samba
- *Betty Carter Album*
- Ornette Coleman
  Skies of America
- John Coltrane
  A Love Supreme
  Meditations
- Chick Corea
  Piano Improvisations Vol.1
- Miles Davis
  Bitches Brew
  Miles Smiles
- Duke Ellington Orchestra
  Far East Suite
- Bill Evans
  Sunday at the Village Vanguard
- João Gilberto
  The Original Bossa Nova Recordings
- Herbie Hancock
  Maiden Voyage
  Headhunters
- *The Electrifying Eddie Harris*
- *The Real Earl Hines*
- Keith Jarrett
  Fort Yaweh

The Köln Concert
- Rahsaan Roland Kirk
  The Inflated Tear
- Steve Lacy
  The Way
- Ramsey Lewis
  The In Crowd
- Jackie McLean
  Let Freedom Ring
- Pat Metheny
  Bright Size Life
- Charles Mingus
  Let My Children Hear Music
- Roscoe Mitchell
  Sound
- Thelonious Monk
  Underground
- Wes Montgomery
  Smokin' at the Half Note
- Joshua Rifkin
  Scott Joplin Piano Rags
- Pee Wee Russell/Coleman Hawkins
  Jazz Reunion
- Günther Schuller
  Jazz Abstractions
- Wayne Shorter
  Night Dreamer
- Jimmy Smith
  Bashin'
- Sun Ra
  The Magic City
- Cecil Taylor
  Unit Structures
- McCoy Tyner
  The Real McCoy
- Grover Washington, Jr.
  Mister Magic
- Weather Report
  Heavy Weather
- Tony Williams
  Emergency
- World Saxophone Quartet
  Revue

5 In all languages (1981–present)

Recent jazz history can seem confusing when we try to grasp the events of greatest historic relevance. Even the early part of the period is still close enough to ensure that changes have not necessarily been fully played out, and the more recent benchmarks can distort a summary view. Hence the need to abandon our strict 20-year demarcations for a 'long score' of a quarter-century plus.

The CD deluge, and more

Variations on established jazz styles, plus a few newly coined (or at least newly named) genres, continued to produce ever more massively documented trails on vinyl, video, cassette tape and such new formats as the compact disc and the digital file. At the same time, the jazz world had to come to terms with the passing of some of its giants.

must know

CD technology provided the continuous, extended playing time that finally made it possible for recorded performances to more closely approximate their live counterparts.

Based solely on the quantity of jazz and jazz-related music that was produced, the period since 1981 threatens to overwhelm. The music's cumulative history was simultaneously being refitted to emerging technology. CD technology, first introduced in 1983, did not change the way jazz was created in the studio as clearly as the advent of the LP, but it did have an impact.

Confirming the classics

An important impact of the CD was the revival it spurred in the sale of jazz recordings. This was a true boon to numerous classic jazz performances, which longtime fans rushed to purchase in the new format and first-time listeners discovered in more pristine digitized sound. Classic jazz labels that had been discontinued by their new corporate owners, including Verve, Blue Note and Impulse!, resurfaced and began to sign new artists, while also re-issuing classics from their catalogue. All of this activity provided a period of greater opportunity for both new stars and young veterans, especially in the late 1980s and early 1990s, although those playing in established styles felt the added burden of competing with the re-issued masterpieces that claimed more and more attention.

A sense of loss

Comparisons between originators and interpreters, always inevitable when dealing with established styles, were underscored in the 1980s by a sense that too many giants were being lost. Ever-present mortality had been balanced in the past to a certain extent by the arrival of new voices with new approaches. As more of the new voices worked in recognizable ways and displayed a growing willingness to acknowledge their sources, the loss of those sources began to feel more ominous. To take the piano as just one example, Bill Evans, Thelonious Monk, Earl Hines,

did you know?

The deaths of legendary musicians threatened to erase a crucial channel of jazz continuity.

Bill Evans's death in 1980 was one of the first signs that the innovators of earlier eras were leaving jazz to younger artists.

Count Basie and Teddy Wilson all died between 1980 and 1986, and their absence (all save Monk were still practising their art) could not help but be felt.

Before the proliferation of high school and college jazz courses, the most reliable way for a young musician to both learn about jazz and establish his or her own profile was to gain employment with an established star. By direct instruction or sheer example, the veteran would provide the means by which the neophyte might attain the necessary tools and personality to make a contribution of his or her own. This form of practical education remained a goal of many young players during the 1980s, but then the death of the four most important bandstand tutors – Art Blakey (1990), Miles Davis (1991), Dizzy Gillespie (1993) and Betty Carter (1998) – foreclosed this critical path to exposure and acceptance.

Coming to terms

As for the new generation of performers, much of its music was overshadowed by debates over where jazz begins and ends, or whether jazz has in fact ended; whether jazz only has value when acknowledging its roots in African American culture, or only continues to advance because non-Americans are applying foreign ideas; and whether catchy names were enough to confirm the creation of new jazz styles. As these arguments, which echoed the small group/big band, traditionalist/beboper, acoustic/electric and straight-ahead/free imbroglios of earlier periods, gained added stridency, it became easier for many to engage the pros and cons of the arguments than the challenges of the music. Still, these debates suggested that this thing called jazz might matter more than had been previously acknowledged.

Deferred ovations

One positive aspect of the recorded deluge, the passing of immortals and the ongoing debates was the opportunity it provided for several brilliant veterans to receive the acclaim and attract the audience that their music had long deserved.

For some – like the composer/pianist Herbie Nichols, who died in 1963 yet only began to receive sustained attention when tribute recordings started to appear in the 1980s – the accolades arrived too late. But many others were able to enjoy the belated attention. Shirley Horn, who had retreated to domestic life after a few notable recordings in the 1960s, returned to establish her soft-spoken vocal style. Tommy Flanagan, a piano stalwart who spent more than a decade accompanying Ella Fitzgerald, finally emerged as a definitive trio stylist. George Coleman, formerly celebrated for little more than his brief tenure with Miles Davis, revealed his virtuosity to a wider world at the head of a quartet. Dave McKenna, yeoman piano accompanist for a host of preboppers, became a reigning solo performer and a definitive interpreter of standards. Jim

Those who had to wait decades for a measure of recognition included singer/pianist Shirley Horn (*left*) and saxophonist George Coleman (*right*).

Joe Henderson confirmed his stature as a dominant jazz voice with a series of well-conceived tribute discs beginning in 1991.

Hall, the soft-spoken electric guitarist known for his warmth and sensitivity, saw his influence reflected in numerous young players and seized the opportunity to expand his career as a leader while also showing his composing and arranging skills. Don Pullen, pigeonholed as part of the avant-garde, brought blues, gospel and more exotic strains to the surface in a variety of settings. Andrew Hill, whose music was seen as straddling tradition and experimentation when it first emerged, added to his legacy with new compositions and new ensembles after returning to activity.

Glorious final acts

Several musicians who had previously received their due, or at least the confirmation that comes via their influence, were also celebrated anew in these years. The most notable example was that of tenor saxophonist Joe Henderson, a star of his own and others' Blue Note records in the 1960s, who first reestablished his power as an influence with his *State of the Tenor* recordings for that label in 1985.

One of Henderson's own early models, Stan Getz, found new creative life at age 60 in 1987 and seized the opportunity until his death four years later to record a series of inspired quartet and duet performances. Benny Carter, finally emerging from the Hollywood studio scene that had claimed his attention for the better part of 40 years, returned to public performance and created a series of orchestral suites, summit meetings (with such younger peers as Dizzy Gillespie and Phil Woods) and small-group sessions that marked him as jazz's most productive octogenarian.

The return of Benny Carter to active performing confirmed that classic jazz remained timeless.

Back to the classics

The new fondness for classic performers, together with the resistance of most pop fans to any music with the least hint of experimentation, created an atmosphere in which a return to classic songs and classic styles appeared to be a promising way to maintain a jazz audience.

At the same time, several notable explorers from previous decades also became more cognizant of what was now often simply designated 'the tradition'. Keith Jarrett, whose ensemble and solo music had focused almost exclusively on original compositions in the previous decade, formed what he designated as his Standards Trio in 1983 with fellow explorers Gary Peacock (bass) and Jack DeJohnette (drums). This enormously popular unit has remained Jarrett's ensemble of choice in the succeeding quarter century. After more than a decade of featuring a

Keith Jarrett (*centre*) reoriented his approach to address standards in a trio with bassist Gary Peacock (*left*) and drummer Jack DeJohnette (*right*).

Charlie Haden was another innovator who turned in a more traditional direction with his Quartet West.

saxophone soloist, McCoy Tyner also reverted to a trio format and began to place a less exclusive focus on original compositions. Bassist Charlie Haden, famed for earlier affiliations with Ornette Coleman and Jarrett, plus his own politically focused Liberation Music Orchestra, turned his attention to moods and music associated with film noir in Quartet West. Without abandoning its celebration of outer space, Sun Ra's Arkestra devoted significant time to skewed takes on Duke Ellington and Fletcher Henderson. Even Ornette Coleman displayed a willingness to look back, at least on occasion, when he reconvened his original Quartet for the acoustic side of the conversation on the 1987 disc *In All Languages* that also featured his electric Prime Time performing many of the same compositions.

Songbook resurgent

As the classic recordings of Louis Armstrong, Ella Fitzgerald, Billie Holiday and others poured forth, listeners began to rediscover (or to discover for the first time) the joys of classic popular standards. Fitzgerald and other still-living legends sustained this surge, none more so than Tony Bennett, who regained and ultimately exceeded his former prominence by making his connection to jazz more pronounced.

Both Harry Connick, Jr, and Diana Krall had originally focused on playing piano before winning fame as vocalists, and both blended a feeling for newer material with an unshakable reverence for the classics. While other young singers followed in their wake, Connick and Krall continued to establish benchmarks for keeping the faith with the vocal tradition.

must know

The rise of younger vocalists, especially Harry Connick, Jr, and Diana Krall, ensured that the Great American Songbook would be a contemporary phenomenon.

Young lions roaring

It was a new generation of jazz instrumentalists, however, that first signalled the coming immersion in the bop-to-modal discoveries of the 1945–1965 modernists. They walked the walk musically (and wore the wardrobe as well), gave hope to those who felt betrayed when John Coltrane championed the free players and Miles Davis switched on, and frustrated those who demanded another new thing. The symbol of this cohort, and of jazz in general as time passed, became trumpeter Wynton Marsalis, one of several musicians from New Orleans who began arriving in New York around 1980. These players and a growing number of their college-age contemporaries were soon christened the Young Lions, and their embrace of acoustic jazz verities that pre-date the tumultuous 1960s was deemed a movement.

New interest in the standard pop songs and jazz vocals was generated by singer/pianists Harry Connick, Jr (*left*) and Diana Krall (*right*).

must know

Harry Connick, Jr, tenor saxophonist Branford Marsalis, trumpeters Terence Blanchard, Wynton Marsalis and Nicholas Payton, and alto saxophonist Donald Harrison are just a few of the many New Orleans musicians who made the journey to New York.

The education generation

The emergence of these musicians was actually the triumph of their teachers – not just other professional musicians, but the actual classroom instructors and childhood mentors who first set them on their paths and provided the necessary jazz fundamentals. One important example is Wynton Marsalis, jazz's most vocal advocate.

did you know?

Wynton Marsalis joined Art Blakey's band in 1980 at the age of 19. A year later he formed his first quintet.

It was the dedication of musician/teachers such as Ellis Marsalis (father of Branford and Wynton), Edward 'Kidd' Jordan and Alvin Batiste as much as any hometown tradition that created the influx of young instrumentalists from New Orleans, and it was other musician/educators, at Berklee College in Boston and the Manhattan School of Music and other programmes around the world, that set young musicians on what some described as their

Pianist, educator and patriarch Ellis Marsalis (*right*) with his second son, trumpeter Wynton Marsalis.

neoclassical course. Jazz education had been taking root with little notice, yet it clearly came into its own in the 1980s. It has remained the single largest producer of new jazz musicians and new listeners to this day. This has been a mixed blessing, as even the most complex jazz techniques have tended to be standardized and disseminated in a manner that has often impeded the development of individual personality. Suddenly dozens of teenagers could play Coltrane's harmonically imposing 'Giant Steps' in every key, though it became harder to tell them apart.

Marsalis's mainstream

Wynton Marsalis has earned his position as jazz's most visible advocate through a command of the trumpet, a simultaneous mastery of classical music that added weight to his musical opinions in the eyes of the non-jazz world, and a dedication to win respect for the music he loved. From the formation of his first quintet, Marsalis made it a point to seek out school-aged musicians and draw them to jazz music. His own source points evolved from the 1960s-era Miles Davis quintet through Louis Armstrong and even earlier New Orleans models to the more expansive creations of Duke Ellington. After affiliating with New York's Lincoln Center, in what began as a summer concert programme in 1987 but had grown into the permanent Jazz at Lincoln Center operation by 1991, Marsalis found uncommon opportunities to realize the epic, multidisciplinary works that even Ellington found too often confined to dreams. In 1997 the trumpeter's sprawling orchestral opus 'Blood on the Fields' captured the Pulitzer Prize that Ellington had been denied.

Wynton Marsalis's command of the trumpet in both jazz and classical settings was a key component in the growing acceptance of jazz as 'serious' music.

A place at the table

For all his talents, Wynton Marsalis also had timing on his side. He appeared at the moment that jazz was finally poised for acceptance as the most serious and satisfying of art forms. In 1982 the National Endowment for the Arts presented the first of what would become annual Jazz Masters awards to the music's premier musicians (Roy Eldridge, Dizzy Gillespie and Sun Ra made up the inaugural class), and in 1987 Representative John Conyers won enactment for a congressional resolution declaring jazz 'a rare and valuable American national treasure'. This was the period in which jazz legends received iconic portrayals as tragic heroes in the films *Round Midnight* (1986, with Dexter Gordon as a character based on both Lester Young and Bud Powell) and *Bird* (Clint Eastwood's 1988 life of Charlie Parker). In 2001, the Smithsonian Institution designated April as Jazz Appreciation Month, a celebration that annually inspires tens of thousands of special events around the world. Suddenly jazz was a mark of American pride and achievement, something that all educated musicians should know how to play and any educated person should appreciate. Even advertisers, who had maintained their distance from the music far longer than Hollywood, found jazz to be the perfect soundtrack for selling everything from coffee to luxury cars.

Competitive jazz

Thelonious Monk provided the best gauge of how secure jazz had become in the cultural realm. But a consensus remained harder to reach regarding styles that had blossomed in the 1960s.

In 1986, four years after Monk's death, the Thelonious Monk Institute of Jazz was formed, with the intention of serving as a jazz counterpart to the Beethoven Society. The annual competition that the Monk Institute began to sponsor for young instrumentalists and singers quickly provided the most visible sign of early acceptance in the name of a man once viewed as the music's ultimate outcast. The wealth of budding talent in the early years of the competition gave the prize added cachet, and pianists Marcus Roberts (1987) and Jacky Terrasson (1993) and saxophonist Joshua Redman (1991) received lavish praise for their victories that their later careers have confirmed.

must know

The Monk Competition has revealed a level of respect for jazz musicians comparable to that long granted their classical counterparts.

Marcus Roberts won the Thelonious Monk Institute of Jazz's first piano competition.

France's Jacky Terrasson, another Monk Competition victor, gave further proof that jazz had become an international language.

After several years in retirement, Miles Davis returned to performing in 1981 and proved to be as popular as ever.

Miles of music

Miles Davis was the most visible bell-wether of the success of styles from the 1960s. The paragon of jazz charisma until his death, the trumpeter remained universally revered for the music he created in the first 20 years of his career (with his 1959 album *Kind of Blue* ascending to a permanent best-selling Valhalla) yet highly controversial for his rock-oriented electric music. From the perspective of Jazz at Lincoln Center, these later efforts had abandoned jazz and were not worthy of the appellation, yet an even larger contingent celebrated all of Davis's music. This latter group included an impressive cross-section of trumpeters, from AACM veteran Wadada Leo Smith, Wallace Roney (another Art Blakey discovery who grew personally and stylistically close to Davis over time) and the younger Dave Douglas (whose ambitious forays into diverse settings made him something of Wynton Marsalis's counterculture counterpart) to such one-time Marsalis acolytes as Roy Hargrove and Nicholas Payton.

The music Davis made after returning from a six-year sabbatical in 1981 is better remembered for the young players he featured (including alto saxophonist Kenny Garrett and electric bassist Marcus Miller) than its own inherent qualities – the 1986 *Tutu*, where studio advances basically allowed Miller to serve as a one-man substitute for Gil Evans's orchestrations being a notable exception. Davis's earlier electric music, however, and his unwillingness to rest on proven approaches, continue to fascinate several jazz generations.

Six-string inventions

Guitar players who drew inspiration from rock and blues as well as jazz were another point of controversy, despite growing numbers and an upper echelon of notably talented players. While Davis's own last bands gave career boosts to two of the best, Mike Stern and John Scofield, another pair who emerged from Boston's Berklee College and never played with the trumpeter offered the clearest examples of how jazz players could operate comfortably in multiple realms. Pat Metheny sustained the popularity of his Metheny Group with an emphasis on accessible melody and touches of folk, Brazilian and even ambient music. Then he tested his fan base with trios that swung in the traditional manner, bucolic duet conversations with Jim Hall and Charlie Haden and unconditional embraces of such avant-garde partners as Ornette Coleman and British free guitar guru Derek Bailey. Bill Frisell cut a similarly wide path, in a longstanding trio led by drummer Paul Motian that also featured Joe Lovano's tenor sax, on special projects with songwriter Burt Bacharach and country music giants, and in numerous working ensembles of his own that defined a new, skewed vision of musical Americana.

Marcus Miller was one of the new stars to emerge from Miles Davis's 1980s' ensembles.

Pat Metheny became a popular phenomenon with his Pat Metheny Group but still found time for more traditional and experimental interludes.

Forms of freedom

Jazz's more abstract wing retained its avant-garde status, despite a basic rhythmic and tonal vocabulary that had been employed for nearly half a century. Much of the most satisfying new music of the period was created in mid-size ensembles, while some new figures rose to prominence in alternative circles.

Julius Hemphill, a founding member of the World Saxophone Quartet and its most important composer, founded his own saxophone sextet after leaving the WSQ in 1990.

To a great extent, practitioners of new music showed the greater inclination towards compositional detail that had been one product of the AACM and those who followed. The blend of structure and improvisation served the World Saxophone Quartet (WSQ) particularly well, especially prior to the 1990 departure of the group's primary composer, Julius Hemphill. Even before Hemphill's exit, the WSQ had begun working with occasional guests and varying their repertoire, creating a body of work that ultimately included tributes to Duke Ellington, Miles Davis and Jimi Hendrix as well as programmes of African music and rhythm and blues. ROVA covered an even greater terrain through frequent commissions of outside composers and its own settings of Coltrane's later music, while Hemphill formed his own saxophone sextet and continued to write brilliant music until his death in 1995.

Mid-size majesty

Mid-size ensembles offered a new range of colours while avoiding both the economic burden of a full orchestra and the limitations such bands place on ensemble interaction. The most rewarding of the

OPPOSITE: A golden era of midsize ensembles was ignited by the work of David Murray (*top*) and Henry Threadgill (*bottom*).

several groups appearing under David Murray's name was an octet that employed declarative writing as a spur to a number of talented soloists, while Chicagoan Edward Wilkinson's Eight Bold Souls confirmed the writing and improvising prowess of the AACM's younger generation.

Henry Threadgill, an earlier AACM product who first gained attention as saxophonist and primary composer in the trio Air, proceeded through the period with several iconoclastic groupings. They included his Sextette (which actually contained seven musicians, including a cellist and two drummers), the even more eccentric Very Very Circus (with two electric guitars and two tubas among its seven pieces) and such twenty-first-century offerings as Make a Move (quintet with electric guitar and electric bass plus vibes) and Zooid (sextet with cello, tuba and oud).

Dutch iconoclasts Willem Breuker in his Kollektief and Misha Mengelberg in his similarly mid-sized ICP Orchestra included more classical allusions and outright parody alongside free episodes. Clarinetist John Carter created the period's most profound music in his *Roots and Folklore* cycle of five album-length suites. Carter's music and his octet made space for every imaginable sound, from muted brass to synthesizers and even recorded oral histories. This epic work drew little attention at the time and remains to be widely appreciated more than a decade after Carter's 1991 death.

Downtown and underground

Some jazz experimenters became known as 'downtown' musicians, a reference that both

must know

John Carter's Pulitzer-worthy *Roots and Folklore* cycle presents a musical history of black people, from pre-slavery days in Africa to modern urban America.

While the jazz tradition was celebrated at New York's Lincoln Center, John Zorn kept the alternative fires burning in lower Manhattan.

located the Manhattan clubs that welcomed them and signalled a clear distance from the uptown proprieties of Lincoln Center. Butch Morris used hand gestures and a system of cues to lead sundry configurations of instruments through improvised 'conductions'. Composer and alto saxophonist John Zorn created similar 'game' pieces such as 'Cobra', while also giving priority to high-decibel distortion with his Naked City group, placing Hebraic melodies in a context recalling early Ornette Coleman in his Masada quartet, and blending extreme textures in original film music. William Parker, a bassist with enormous sound and drive, became perhaps the most ubiquitous of the free players through several ongoing affiliations (with saxophonist David S. Ware, pianist Matthew Shipp and drummer Hamid Drake), his own various quartets and Little Huey Creative Music Orchestra. Drummer Bobby Previte's writing suggested minimalism and rock as well as jazz, while another percussionist, Ronald Shannon Jackson, graduated from Coleman's Prime Time to the avant-rock of his own Decoding Society.

must know

Established in 1996, the annual Vision Festival is now the major New York new jazz event.

A world of connections

Given the limited audience for new music, most downtown players had to create multiple musical settings, which in turn allowed new combinations that frequently drew inspiration from other cultures and styles. Some new approaches found more audience acceptance than others.

Trumpeter Dave Douglas became one of the most prolific and prominent of these players. He played with an array of bands that included a quintet dominated by stringed instruments that mixed originals with covers of contemporary classical works, the Tiny Bell Trio with a focus on Balkan music, Charms of the Night Sky with violin and accordion among its four pieces, as well as more conventional quartets and sextets. Pianist Uri Caine, a frequent Douglas associate, employed turntable-manipulating deejays and Hebrew cantors to open Mahler, Bach, Beethoven and Mozart to contemporary improvisation and re-imagined instrumental pop with the electric trio Bedrock, with occasional forays into acoustic trio and solo performance. Don Byron's clarinet paid homage to klezmer and cartoon music, employed the Latin inflected Music for Six Musicians to accompany rap and political protest, embraced art songs and celebrated the legacies of Lester Young and Motown's Junior Walker. For these musicians and others, diversity became a central feature of their profile.

Dave Douglas applied his creative curiosity in a wide variety of ensembles.

International envoys

Jazz and its offshoots continue to exist and often thrive in other parts of the world, and the importance

The impact of musicians from the Caribbean such as Cuba's Paquito D'Rivera ushered in a new era of dialogue between jazz and Latin music.

of musicians from countries other than the United States has remained on a steady upswing. Many have come from Cuba, including Paquito D'Rivera (alto sax and clarinet), Arturo Sandoval (trumpet) and Jesus 'Chucho' Valdes, all of whom first became prominent in the band Irakere before gaining fame as leaders outside their homeland. Pianist Gonzalo Rubalcaba and drummer Dafnis Prieto represent a younger Cuban contingent.

Other Caribbean countries produced such jazz stars as pianists Michel Camilo (Dominican Republic) and Danilo Perez (Panama) and saxophonist David Sanchez (Puerto Rico), each of whom blended homeland influences into their concepts. South African Abdullah Ibrahim became the voice in exile of his homeland's liberation struggle in the 1980s with his septet Ekaya before turning to a trio focus, while Tunisian oud player Anour Brahem began working with jazz pianists and rhythm sections.

In search of the new

The hunger for new trends, or newly coined labels for musical approaches, was most obvious in such momentary movements as klezmer jazz, acid jazz (an earlier dance-oriented iteration launched in Britain during the 1980s) and neo-swing (a blend of 1930s horn riffs and r&b sustained during its brief life by television commercials for a clothing store). A group of young musicians living in Brooklyn during the 1980s made a conscious effort to originate their own blend of funk and advanced jazz playing under the rubric M-BASE.

While alto saxophonist Steve Coleman has worked most consistently within the M-BASE

must know

Many groups in Europe, influenced by contemporary dance music, have embraced ambient sound and sonic manipulation. For some, these hybrids are truer to the spirit of jazz than the more tradition-focused alternatives.

parameters, his alto playing counterpart Greg Osby and vocalist Cassandra Wilson have built styles of their own at once both individualistic and closer to jazz orthodoxy, with Osby serving as mentor to such younger figures as pianist Jason Moran and vibraphonist Stefon Harris. Another new designation, 'jam band', denotes an array of groups that play primarily in alternative rock settings and emphasize lengthy solos over dance beats. Some, like the trio Medeski Martin and Wood, possess grounding in the jazz and avant-garde traditions, while many others draw their inspiration from the Jimmy Smith organ combo model or more open-ended rock icons like The Grateful Dead and Santana.

Cassandra Wilson moved from her experimental jazz base to create a personal sound that met with great popular success.

Striking up the bland

Like any music that demands attentive listening for full appreciation, jazz has often found itself crowded out by hybrids that replace challenge with a bland background impersonality. Such was the case in the early 1980s, when the spare, monochromatic improvisations of New Age pianists and guitarists had their moment. The phenomenon called smooth jazz has proven more sturdy and, given its name, highly misleading. With Kenny G's soprano sax curlicues as its signature sound, smooth jazz has become far more accessible to the average listener than more substantial styles of jazz. While several talented players have been lumped into the smooth category, including guitarist Earl Klugh and saxophonist Kirk Whalum, the majority of what passes for smooth jazz has little or no real jazz content.

Earl Klugh was one of the few artists who brought substance to 'smooth' jazz.

must know

The term 'smooth jazz' was coined by radio consultants seeking a new adult music format that offered an unthreatening blend of rock, jazz and soul.

Old and new notables

All of this activity produced a number of new jazz stars, some of whom were working across the music's various factions to craft original work. A short but by no means complete sampling indicates the wealth of talent involved.

Joe Lovano paid dues in other folks' bands for more than a decade before emerging as one of the jazz world's leading figures in the 1990s.

Some had received their jazz education in the 1960s (trumpeter Tom Harrell) and 1970s (saxophonist Joe Lovano, pianist Kenny Werner) and had to wait longer to have their own music heard. Lovano in particular has proven to be an improvising and conceptual powerhouse, with bands that celebrate Italian opera, Fifty Second Street bebop pioneers, the jazz/classical Third Stream fusion, and Frank Sinatra. After a decade in support of Miles Davis, Anthony Braxton and Sam Rivers, British bassist Dave Holland formed one exceptional quintet in the 1980s and another in the 1990s, then added seven pieces for occasional and equally rewarding forays into the big band realm. The Gonzalez brothers Andy (bass) and Jerry (trumpet and conga drums) parlayed the exposure to both jazz and Afro-Latin music that they received while growing up in the Bronx and formed the Fort Apache band, which underscored the deep affinities between modern jazz and Latin rhythms.

Several pianists have reinvigorated the trio format, with varying emphases on the postbop mainstream (Mulgrew Miller), Romanticism and alternative pop (Brad Mehldau), Broadway and cabaret (Bill Charlap) and the more iconoclastic voices of jazz's past (Geri Allen). The tenor sax plus rhythm quartet continued to dominate, with strong

The diverse strengths of jazz in the late twentieth century were epitomized by powerhouse saxophonist George Adams (*left*), composer Maria Schneider (*top*) and veteran Clark Terry (*below*).

ties to the examples of Monk (Sphere), Mingus (George Adams/Don Pullen Quartet) and Coltrane (Quest, Michael Brecker, Branford Marsalis). Maria Schneider carried the orchestral torch for her mentors Bob Brookmeyer and the late Gil Evans with her own orchestra, while Argentinian Guillermo Klein created a new manner of jazz/Hispanic synthesis.

With all these younger figures in ascendance, there was still room for Wayne Shorter, who introduced a bold new acoustic quartet in 2001, and the astoundingly active veterans Dave Brubeck, Roy Haynes, Sonny Rollins and Clark Terry to remain among jazz's most popular figures.

Jazz beyond the twentieth century

After a century in which it has contributed more to musical culture than any other style worldwide, jazz continues to elude a fixed meaning. Having attained a level of respect equivalent to that of other 'art' musics, it remains vulnerable to changing tastes, general indifference and the tyranny of the bottom line. The nightclub, its primary home for most of the music's history, is similarly endangered, and the opportunity to hear jazz on the radio and purchase it in recorded formats is also undergoing significant transformations. As more and more discussions about all forms of creative art begin and end with what sells and what does not, jazz is not in a position of strength.

Singer/pianist Norah Jones includes hints of jazz in her music, though her great success is tied more clearly to the singer/songwriter tradition of recent pop music.

Alto saxophonist Kenny Garrett (*right*, with Guru/Jazzmatazz) is among the jazz soloists who have attempted to seek a merger with hiphop.

Yet predicting the future of jazz or any music is a tricky business. Who in the year 2000 would have anticipated that in a mere five years something called an iPod would have been leading towards the demise of the compact disc? And who, in an earlier era, would have envisioned Armstrong and Monk on postage stamps? A jazz musician may never again enjoy the mass adulation that greeted Benny Goodman in 1936, but as an approach for spontaneous collective sonic creation, jazz retains a power and a universal appeal that mark it as the first and most inclusive example of 'world' music. The impact jazz has had on popular, classical and ethnic musics in its first century suggests that it will continue to inspire and blend with other styles, which will only make the task of definition harder; yet the spirit and substance of jazz's greatest creators appears substantial enough to withstand any further mutations.

While some musicians push in more electric and processed directions, Branford Marsalis remains committed to acoustic music.

want to know more?

The albums listed below, along with the musicians or groups who performed them, are some of the highlights of the era.

- **George Adams/Don Pullen Quartet**
  Live at the Village Vanguard, Vol. 2
- **Michael Brecker**
  Tales from the Hudson
- **Uri Caine**
  Urlicht: Primal Light
- **Betty Carter**
  Feed the Fire
- **John Carter**
  Castles of Ghana
- **Bill Charlap**
  Written in the Stars
- **George Coleman**
  Manhattan Panorama
- **Ornette Coleman**
  In All Languages
- **Steve Coleman**
  The Sonic Language of Myth
- **Harry Connick, Jr**
  Come by Me
- **Miles Davis**
  Tutu
- **Dave Douglas**
  Convergence
- **Paquito D'Rivera**
  Portraits of Cuba
- **Tommy Flanagan**
  Sea Changes
- **Fort Apache Band**
  Rumba para Monk
- **Bill Frisell**
  Have a Little Faith
- **Jim Hall**
  Textures
- **Julius Hemphill Sextet**
  Fat Man and the Hard Blues
- **Andrew Hill**
  Dusk
- **Shirley Horn**
  You Won't Forget Me
- **Abdullah Ibrahim**
  Water from an Ancient Well
- **ICP Orchestra**
  Jubilee Varia
- **Keith Jarrett**
  Up for It
- **Diana Krall**
  Love Scenes
- **Joe Lovano**
  Rush Hour
- **Branford Marsalis**
  Eternal
- **Wynton Marsalis**
  Blood on the Fields
- **Dave McKenna**
  Shadows 'n' Dreams
- **Medeski Martin & Wood**
  Shack-man
- **Brad Mehldau**
  House on Hill
- **Pat Metheny**
  The Way Up
- **David Murray**
  New Life
- **Greg Osby**
  Art Forum
- **Joshua Redman**
  MoodSwing
- **Sonny Rollins**
  G-Man
- **Gonzalo Rubalcaba**
  Paseo
- **John Scofield**
  EnRoute
- **Sphere**
  Four for All
- **Henry Threadgill**
  You Know the Number
- **Cassandra Wilson**
  New Moon Daughter
- **John Zorn**
  The Big Gundown

Glossary

acid jazz jazz with an emphasis on funk, which became popular in British dance clubs during the 1980s

bebop modern jazz, as represented originally by Dizzy Gillespie and Charlie Parker; the term is taken from one of Gillespie's compositions

blue notes the flatted third and flatted seventh in the major scale – for example, Eb and Bb in the key of C major

blues a musical style that usually involves a twelve-bar chorus and AAB structure, and music of related mood and form

bop *see* bebop

bossa nova variation on the samba pioneered in Brazil by composer Antonio Carlos Jobim and vocalist João Gilberto, and popularized in the United States by Stan Getz and others

cakewalk a high-stepping dance, popular in the United States at the end of the nineteenth century, that originated on southern plantations when slaves mimicked the affectations of plantation owners

call-and-response the process by which a musical phrase, stated by one instrument or section of an ensemble, is repeated or responded to by another; commonly used in jazz arrangements

circle dances dances performed by dancers arranged in a circle; *see also* ring shouts

contemporary jazz usually connotes the more commercial, pop-inflected forms of jazz that have arisen in the past two decades, though applicable to any jazz created by contemporary musicians

cool jazz a style, sometimes referred to as 'West Coast', characterized by light, vibrato-free instrumental tones; the use of orchestral instruments such as flute, French horn and tuba that were previously more closely associated with classical music; and an emphasis on counterpoint and other supposedly 'classical' techniques

Dixieland often used as a pejorative to connote a simplified and commercialized version of the traditional jazz style, but also employed to describe any jazz in the style originally developed in New Orleans

downtown musicians avant-garde and other experimental musicians associated with the Knitting Factory and other lower Manhattan clubs during and after the late 1980s

East Coast jazz a style, sometimes referred to as 'hard bop', characterized by a focus on the blues and standard song forms, strong and interactive drum and piano accompaniment, and extended improvisations in which feeling (or 'soul') is as valued as virtuosity

free jazz an avant-garde style that stresses in various combinations irregular structures that don't rely on recurring harmonies but may employ extreme instrumental sounds, flexible rhythms and textures, and unusual ensemble configurations

fusion the merger of jazz and rock or, more generally, the synthesis of any two distinct musical styles

hard bop *see* East Coast jazz

head arrangement an arrangement generated spontaneously by members of an ensemble and committed to memory, as opposed to being translated to a written score

jam bands bands with pop and alternative-rock foundations that featured long improvisational passages; the term gained popularity in the late 1990s

jass early spelling of 'jazz'

Jazz Age a period in United States history lasting roughly from the end of World War I (1918) to the beginning of the Great Depression (1929) that saw the early rise and spread of jazz music; has been identified with hedonism as described in the works of novelist F. Scott Fitzgerald

jungle music music created by Duke Ellington's orchestra for floorshows at Harlem's Cotton Club in the late 1920s

kicks bands ensembles (usually big bands) that assembled and performed for the joy of playing specific music rather than for any anticipated monetary gain; the term gained popularity in the 1960s

modern jazz the style created in New York City during the early 1940s, also known as bebop

neo-swing a hybrid of big-band swing and rhythm and blues that enjoyed brief popularity in the late 1990s

open form musical structures that do not provide fixed harmonic resolution, but instead remain 'open' to allow improvisers to extend their statements at will

playing the changes conforming to the harmonic structure (or 'chord changes') of a song when improvising

race records recordings produced specifically for the African American audience; the term gained currency in the 1920s

ragtime a composed piano music featuring distinct sections usually of 16 bars and staggered, 'ragged' syncopated melodies

rent party parties held in homes or apartments in Harlem and other African American communities in the first half of the twentieth century, in which tenants charged a fee (and thus raised rent money) and provided live music and other entertainment

ring shouts a variation of the circle dance; arose among African Americans during the Civil War period and included several facets (blue notes, improvisation, call-and-response) later identified with jazz

scat singing improvised wordless vocals

slap-tongue technique an overly heavy use of the tongue in articulating a note on the saxophone, producing an initial pop or 'slap' sound

smooth jazz a radio format, used to describe instrumental pop music or vocal pop music with a strong instrumental component; the term first appeared in the late 1980s

stride piano early jazz piano style in which the left hand 'strides' between bass notes and higher supporting chords while accompanying melodic lines in the right hand

traditional jazz the style of jazz performed in New Orleans in the first decades of the twentieth century, characterized by small ensembles featuring cornet or trumpet, trombone, clarinet, banjo, tuba and drums that emphasize polyphony and group (as opposed to individual) improvisation

***vodun* societies** religious groups found in New Orleans and Havana through which displaced Africans met to retain their religious practices

West Coast jazz *see* cool jazz

Need to know more?

If you would like to delve deeper into the world of jazz, there is a wealth of information available about the musicians and styles discussed in this book. Listed below are some useful websites, magazines and other resources.

Websites

www.smithsonianjazz.org
A Smithsonian Institution website that provides a complete international listing of events scheduled to honour jazz during April, Jazz Appreciation Month, and a lot of other information on jazz for fans, teachers, and students.

www.jazzhouse.org
Maintained by the Jazz Journalists Association – includes print and photo archives, obituaries and results of the organization's annual awards poll.

www.jazzcorner.com
Provides links to numerous sites of individual musicians and bands.

www.pointofdeparture.org
Emphasizes new music.

www.jerryjazzmusician.com
Dedicated to jazz and American culture, featuring interviews, reminiscences and recommendations for listening.

www.jazzdiscography.com
Displays work by several discographers, with an emphasis on modern musicians.

www.jazzdisco.org
A discography site that provides information on labels as well as on individual musicians.

www.lordisco.com
A complete CD-ROM jazz discography produced by Tom Lord.

Magazines

Several magazines are devoted to jazz, and each also maintains a website.

Down Beat
www.downbeat.com

JazzTimes
www.jazztimes.com

Jazziz
www.jazziz.com
Includes a sample CD in every issue.

Cadence
www.cadencebuilding.com
The most comprehensive source for reviews of new recordings.

All About Jazz
www.allaboutjazz.com/newyork
The New York edition of this magazine includes schedules for the numerous live jazz performances in the city.

Signal to Noise

www.signaltonoisemagazine.org*Coda*

www.coda1958.com

A Canadian journal with a jazz focus.

Swing Journal

www.swingjournal.co.jp

A jazz magazine from Japan.

The Wire

www.thewire.co.uk

A British publication that emphasizes all styles of innovative music.

Radio stations

You can hear jazz on many radio stations around the world. These are two stations with an emphasis on jazz that are also available on the Internet:

WBGO-FM

Based in Newark, New Jersey

www.wbgo.org

KKJZ-FM

Based in Long Beach, California

www.jazzandblues.org/index/aspx

Books

Several essential volumes for a basic jazz library are available in paperback from Oxford University Press. They include:

Feather, Leonard, and Ira Gitler, *The Biographical Encyclopedia of Jazz* (2000)

Hasse, John Edward, ed., *Jazz: The First Century* (2001)

Kernfeld, Barry, ed., *The New Grove Dictionary of Jazz* (2001)

Kirchner, Bill, ed., *The Oxford Companion to Jazz* (2005)

Schuller, Gunther, *Early Jazz* (1968)

Schuller, Gunther, *The Swing Era* (1999)

Stearns, Marshall, *The Story of Jazz* (1970)

Williams, Martin, *The Jazz Tradition*, 2nd rev. edn (1993)

Also noteworthy:

Hodeir, Andre, *Jazz: Its Evolution and Essence* (Grove Press, updated 1980) Currently hard to find but highly recommended.

Other resources

The Smithsonian Institution is currently at work on a revised edition of the out-of-print *Smithsonian Collection of Classic Jazz*. The new album, *Jazz: The Smithsonian Anthology*, will include six CDs and will be issued by Smithsonian Folkways recordings.

Index

AACM 141–2, 176
Adderley, Cannonball 11, 105, 122, 124, 134, 147
Allen, Red 37, 47, 52, 62
Ammons, Gene 79, 106, 108
Armstrong, Louis 8, 11, 24, 32–42, 44–7, 50, 62, 76, 82, 116, 137
Ayler, Albert 129, 139–40, 158
Basie, Count 5, 6, 64–5, 68, 88, 110–12, 131, 134, 164
bebop 80–5
Bechet, Sidney 24, 29, 38, 52, 54, 69, 116–17, 123
Beiderbecke, Bix 34, 44–5, 60, 90
Benson, George 152, 158
Bigard, Barney 54–6, 112
Blakey, Art 9, 102, 105, 134, 164
blues 5, 19–20, 37–8
Bolden, Buddy 23–4
Braxton, Anthony 142, 146, 155–6
Brown, Clifford 79, 102, 104
Brown, Ray 75, 87, 101
Brubeck, Dave 100–1, 132, 134, 183
Calloway, Cab 55, 61, 63, 82, 88–9
Carter, Benny 37, 50, 98, 158, 166
Carter, Betty 79, 148, 164
Carter, John 177
Chicago 26, 27, 33–4, 39, 41
Clarke, Kenny 67, 81, 92, 101
Cole, Nat King 77, 78
Coleman, Ornette 9, 120–1, 138, 140, 155, 168, 175
Coltrane, John 94, 103, 106–7, 122–4, 130–1, 137
Condon, Eddie 34, 69, 82, 115
cool jazz 96–101
Corea, Chick 146, 156
Cotton Club 55–6
Dameron, Tadd 75, 93
Davis, Miles 11, 81, 82, 93, 95–6, 102–3, 109, 122, 134, 145–7, 153–5, 164, 174–5
Dodds, Johnny 24, 33, 39, 41

Dorsey, Jimmy 43, 61, 66
Dorsey, Tommy 43, 61–2, 69–70
Eicher, Manfred 153–4
Eldridge, Roy 69, 115, 117, 158, 172
Ellington, Duke 11, 53–7, 86, 110, 112–13, 131, 132, 149
Europe, James Reese 28, 29
Evans, Bill 122, 124, 136–7, 148, 163
Evans, Gil 97, 109, 122, 148, 174
Fitzgerald, Ella 77, 87–8, 134, 148, 165, 168
free jazz/fusion 129, 138–44
Garner, Erroll 96
Getz, Stan 96, 108, 132–3, 151, 166
Gillespie, "Dizzy" 67, 77, 81–4, 88, 90, 97, 101, 106–7, 132, 164, 172
Giuffre, Jimmy 99, 138
Goodman, Benny 6, 7, 11, 34, 60–1, 68
Gordon, Dexter 79, 142, 157, 172
Granz, Norman 86–9, 148
Hampton, Lionel 62–4, 78–9, 158
Hancock, Herbie 134, 145–6, 158
Handy, W.C. 20, 25, 28–9, 116, 158
hard bop 96, 102–7, 134
Hardin, Lil 33, 35, 39
Hawkins, Coleman 35, 36, 50, 62, 69, 80, 82, 85, 88, 115, 117, 131, 134
Hell Fighters 28, 29
Henderson, Fletcher 7, 35–7, 60, 66, 168
Henderson, Joe 9, 166
Herman, Woody 86, 108, 134, 148
Hines, Earl 40, 41, 77, 81, 136, 163
Hodges, Johnny 112–13
Holiday, Billie 49, 67, 88, 91, 117, 168
Jacquet, Illinois 79, 86, 97, 110, 158
Jarrett, Keith 154, 167
Jobim, Carlos 132, 133

Johnson, "Bunk" 69, 114
Johnson, J.J. 81, 109, 111
Johnson, James P. 18, 26, 48, 53
Jones, Elvin 123, 130, 139, 145
Joplin, Scott 14, 19, 29, 157
Jordan, Louis 78
Kenton, Stan 89, 98, 109, 134
Keppard, Freddie 24, 26
Kirk, Roland 135
Konitz, Lee 94, 97, 109, 157
Krall, Diana 168–9
Krupa, Gene 34, 60, 62, 90
Lewis, John 75, 97, 101, 133
Lunceford, Jimmie 58, 61
Machito 88–9
Marable, Fate 32–3, 34
Marsalis, Branford 169–70, 183
Marsalis, Wynton 10, 169–72, 174
McLean, Jackie 105, 138–9
Mengelberg, Misha 142, 177
Metheny, Pat 154–5, 175
Miller, Glenn 61, 62, 69, 74
Mingus, Charlie 79, 90, 118–19, 120, 131, 138, 158
MJQ 101, 133
modal jazz 122–4
Monk, Thelonius 81–2, 93–4. 123, 136, 163, 173
Montgomery, Wes 79, 134–5, 151
Morton, Jelly Roll 14, 18–19, 25–6, 51–2
Mulligan, Gerry 96–9
Murray, David 177
Navarro, Fats 75, 93
New Orleans 4, 14–16, 21–6, 32
New Orleans Rhythm Kings 34, 52
Oliver, King 8, 14–15, 24, 26, 32, 34, 37, 44, 51–2
Original Dixieland Jazzband 14, 20, 22, 25, 27–9
Ory, Kid 24, 26, 32, 39, 114
Parker, Charlie 9, 70, 77, 80–6, 88–91, 95, 97, 101, 108
Peterson, Oscar 87, 88, 134

Powell, Bud 81, 90–2
Ragtime 18–19, 157
Rainey, Ma 20
Red Hot Peppers 51–2
Redman, Don 36–7, 57
Reinhardt, Django 50–1
Roach, Max 81–2, 85, 90, 102, 104–5, 131, 158
Rogers, Shorty 96, 98
Rollins, Sonny 94, 103–7, 138, 158, 183
Russell, "Pee Wee" 62, 69, 134
Shorter, Wayne 105, 147, 183
Silver, Horace 103, 105, 134
Sinatra, Frank 70, 76–7, 91, 134, 148
Singleton, Zutty 35, 52, 62
Smith, Bessie 38
Stewart, Rex 37, 45, 112
Sun Ra 121, 128, 138, 168, 172
swing 59–70
Tatum, Art 67, 80, 95
Taylor, Cecil 119–20, 121, 138, 140, 158
Taylor, Creed 151–2
Teagarden, Jack 59, 62, 116
Terrasson, Jacky 173–4
Third Stream 133
Tristano, Lennie 94–5
Tyner, McCoy 123, 130, 139, 145, 157, 168
Van Gelder, Rudy 106–7, 152
Vaughan, Sarah 77, 148
Waller, Fats 4, 11, 48–9, 63, 67, 116
Washington, Dinah 77, 79
Washington, Grover 152
Weather Report 147
Webb, Chick 57–8, 61, 78, 87
Webster, Ben 57, 82, 88, 117
Whiteman, Paul 42–3, 59, 68
Williams, Tony 134, 146
Wilson, Teddy 49, 62, 64, 164
World Saxophone Quartet 156–7, 176
Young, Lester 66–7, 69, 80, 83, 85, 88, 90–1, 98, 101, 108, 110, 117